Praise for You *Might Be a Zombie and Other Bad News*

"Hugely enjoyable. I found it irresistible but, sadly, too useful by far."

—Noel Botham, chairman of the Useless Information Society and author of *The Book of Useless Information*

"Trivia on steroids! A wild, irreverent ride through some of the craziest facts I've ever come across, and that's really saying something. I read it straight through."

—Don Voorhees, author of *The Book of Totally Useless Information*

"A hugely enjoyable read—witty, well researched, and worth buying for 'Five Stories About Jesus's Childhood They Had to Cut from the Bible' alone."

—Karl Shaw, author of *5 People Who Died During Sex*

"This book blows the lid off dozens of absurd fallacies and unearths scores of highly entertaining historical ironies."

—Joey Green, author of *Contrary to Popular Belief*

SHOCKING BUT UTTERLY TRUE FACTS!

FROM THE EDITORS OF CRACKED

Michael O'Mara Books Limited

First published in the US by Plume, a member of the Penguin Group (USA) Inc.
First published in Great Britain in 2014 by
Michael O'Mara Books Limited
9 Lion Yard
Tremadoc Road
London SW4 7NQ

Published by arrangement with Plume, a member of Penguin Group (USA) LLC

A CIP catalogue record for this book is available from the British Library.

Papers used by Michael O'Mara Books Limited are natural, recyclable products made from wood grown in sustainable forests. The manufacturing processes conform to the environmental regulations of the country of origin.

ISBN: 978-1-78243-320-0 in paperback print format
ISBN: 978-1-78243-330-9 in e-book format

1 2 3 4 5 6 7 8 9 10

www.mombooks.com

Designed by Spring Hoteling

Printed and bound by CPI Group (UK) Ltd, Croydon, CR0 4YY

For refusing to collapse into an earth-devouring black hole under the force of its own staggering density, we dedicate this book to Theodore Roosevelt's left testicle.

CONTENTS

ACKNOWLEDGMENTS
xiii

INTRODUCTION
xv

THE FIVE MOST HORRIFYING BUGS IN THE WORLD
1

THREE COLORS YOU DON'T REALIZE
ARE CONTROLLING YOUR MIND
7

THE FOUR MOST BADASS PRESIDENTS OF ALL TIME
13

FIVE FAMOUS ARTISTS WHO DIDN'T
CREATE THEIR SIGNATURE CREATION
21

SIX TERRIFYING THINGS THEY DON'T
TELL YOU ABOUT CHILDBIRTH
28

FIVE FUN THINGS THAT WILL KILL YOU
34

CONTENTS

FIVE MOVIES BASED ON TRUE STORIES
(THAT ARE COMPLETE BULLSHIT)
41

OH THE PLACES YOU'LL GO (WHEN YOU'RE DEAD):
SIX INSANE THINGS SCIENCE MIGHT DO WITH YOUR CADAVER
49

THE FIVE MOST RIDICULOUS LIES YOU
WERE TAUGHT IN HISTORY CLASS
54

THE SIX CUTEST ANIMALS THAT CAN STILL DESTROY YOU
62

FIVE STORIES ABOUT JESUS'S CHILDHOOD THEY
HAD TO CUT FROM THE BIBLE (TO AVOID AN NC-17 RATING)
71

THE SIX MOST TERRIFYING FOODS IN THE WORLD
79

FIVE WACKY MISUNDERSTANDINGS THAT
ALMOST CAUSED A NUCLEAR HOLOCAUST
86

THE SIX MOST DEPRESSING HAPPY ENDINGS IN MOVIE HISTORY
94

FIVE FAMOUS INVENTORS WHO STOLE THEIR BIG IDEA
102

THE FIVE MOST FREQUENTLY QUOTED BULLSHIT STATISTICS
109

CONTENTS

THE FOUR MOST INSANE ATTEMPTS TO
TURN NATURE INTO A WEAPON
116

THE FOUR GREATEST THINGS EVER ACCOMPLISHED WHILE HIGH
123

FOUR MYTHOLOGICAL BEASTS THAT ACTUALLY EXIST
131

FIVE WAYS YOUR BRAIN IS MESSING WITH YOUR HEAD
138

FIVE FIGHT MOVES THAT ONLY WORK IN MOVIES
146

FIVE AWESOME PLACES TO HAVE SEX
(AND THE HORRIFIC CONSEQUENCES)
151

FIVE AWESOME THINGS YOU DIDN'T KNOW
COULD MAKE YOU SICK
157

FOUR THINGS YOUR MOM SAID WERE
HEALTHY THAT CAN KILL YOU
162

THE GRUESOME ORIGINS OF FIVE POPULAR FAIRY TALES
169

FIVE HORRIFYING FOOD ADDITIVES
YOU'VE PROBABLY EATEN TODAY
176

CONTENTS

FIVE STORIES THE MEDIA DOESN'T
WANT YOU TO KNOW ABOUT
183

FOUR BRAINWASHING TECHNIQUES
THEY'RE USING ON YOU RIGHT NOW
191

FIVE HOLLYWOOD ADAPTATIONS THAT
TOTALLY MISSED THE POINT
197

THE TEN MOST INSANE MEDICAL PRACTICES IN HISTORY
205

FOUR GREAT WOMEN BURIED BY THEIR BOOBS
213

THE AWFUL TRUTH BEHIND FIVE ITEMS
ON YOUR GROCERY LIST
220

FIVE CLASSIC CARTOON CHARACTERS
WITH TRAUMATIC CHILDHOODS
228

FIVE CONSPIRACIES THAT NEARLY BROUGHT
DOWN THE U.S. GOVERNMENT
236

FOUR TICKING TIME BOMBS IN NATURE MORE TERRIFYING
(AND LIKELY) THAN THE ONES IN DISASTER MOVIES
243

CONTENTS

FIVE PSYCHOLOGICAL EXPERIMENTS THAT
PROVE HUMANITY IS DOOMED
249

THE FIVE CREEPIEST URBAN LEGENDS
THAT HAPPEN TO BE TRUE
258

FIVE BELOVED U.S. PRESIDENTS THE MODERN MEDIA
WOULD NEVER LET INTO THE WHITE HOUSE
265

THIRD REICH TO FORTUNE 500:
FIVE POPULAR BRANDS THE NAZIS GAVE US
272

FIVE SCIENTIFIC REASONS WHY A ZOMBIE APOCALYPSE
COULD ACTUALLY HAPPEN
280

CREDITS
289

ACKNOWLEDGMENTS

THE Cracked.com editorial team would like to thank the thousands of talented comedy writers who worked tirelessly, often under threat of violence, to make this book possible.

In addition to the folks listed in the credits section, we would like to thank every last member of the Cracked Writer's Workshop. The Workshop is an ongoing experiment based on the idea that if you let thousands of Internet strangers into your writers' room, some of them will turn out to be geniuses. Others will turn out to be dangerous and deranged, sure, but that was a risk we were willing to take. It paid off—you're holding the proof in your hands. We would also like to thank the effortlessly funny PWoT forum moderators, for cultivating the only online community where such an experiment could be anything but an embarrassing failure.

We're eternally grateful to the illustrators and Randall Maynard, for their ability to draw exactly what we had in our heads, except way better and without all the dicks. Also, to our fact checker Ben Smith, for the hours of Google and library searches that have almost certainly made him a person of interest to the FBI.

A huge thanks to everyone at Demand Media, especially

ACKNOWLEDGMENTS

Larry Fitzgibbon, Jeremy Reed, Stewart Marlborough, and Lex Friedman, for taking a chance on a site that, in retrospect, probably wasn't very good yet, and to Richard Rosenblatt and Shawn Colo, for trusting that it could one day be worth a damn. And, of course, thanks to Cracked.com GM Oren Katzeff, for putting up with us and running a tight ship that features far less sodomy than most in naval history. We'd especially like to thank Mandy Ng, Adam Tourkow, Simon Jia, and Lina Ung, for the incredible work they put in every day to keep Cracked.com up and running. We'd also like to thank Matt Polesetsky, David Ho, and Emma Sansing in the legal department, Wadooah Wali and our PR team, and our SEO, marketing, sales, and monetization teams. Special thanks to Wil Teran, Billy Janes, and the design team for making us look like a real, legitimate website, and to Shannon O'Brien and Moment Design for all the free advice.

We would especially like to thank Becky Cole and Nadia Kashper from Penguin, and our agent Dan Strone from Trident Media Group, for their invaluable feedback, and for giving us the creative license to stray outside of the rules as dictated by the AP (and common decency) when we swore it was necessary.

And of course none of this would be possible without the young men and women who have fought and died so we could go on doing our ridiculous job. We may not know any of your names, but you are the bravest interns in the world.

INTRODUCTION

THE CONSPIRACY

YOU have been the victim of a conspiracy to make the world around you more boring than it actually is.

It's true. Did you know that you could save the lives of thousands of depressed people by painting the Golden Gate Bridge blue? How about the brain parasite currently infecting 50 percent of people on earth that turns lab rats into zombies—did you know about *that*? We didn't think so.

Nearly everything your impressionable mind soaks up from your peers, teachers, parents, and the media is a lie. Imagine if *Pulp Fiction* and *Goodfellas* had been rolled into a single movie and set loose aboard the spaceship from *Aliens*. That's the real world you've been missing. The people who taught you everything you know took that movie, edited out all of the most aggressively ass-kicking scenes, and made it into a Saturday-morning cartoon. This book is the shocking, unrated director's cut.

You hold in your hands the most mind-blowing nuggets of information federal and local anti-headsplosion laws allow us to print on anything that's not a tarp. In these pages, you will find answers to questions you didn't even know you should be asking. Questions like, Why *were* the Nazi's so well dressed? and, Why is this five-inch-long hornet chasing me?

THE ROAD TO *YOU MIGHT BE A ZOMBIE*

The many shocking answers you'll find in this book all arose from a single question we found ourselves asking about two years ago: How can we come up with $2.5 million, and fast?

It didn't take us long to settle on the idea of writing a book. Like our online humor articles, books contain words. But while our website is free, people who suck at shoplifting pay *money* for books. The more we looked into this book business, the more the idea checked out. Our first move was to take a quick survey of some of the bestselling books of all time.

The Bible (300 BC–AD 95), 6 billion copies sold

Quotations from Chairman Mao (1964), 800 million copies sold

The Koran (AD 610–632), 800 million copies sold

Xinhua Dictionary (1957), 400 million copies sold

A number of striking similarities jumped out immediately. In addition to being old as shit, we noticed that all four endeavored to answer some of life's biggest questions. After literally hours of brainstorming, we sent off the first draft of our book proposal and began taking out sizable loans and buying tiny expensive jets (to serve as fuel for our larger, also expensive, jets). Unfortunately, some guy named Webster had somehow retroactively stolen our idea "What Words Mean" and had even found definitions for real words rather than ones he'd just made up. After follow-up calls with publishing houses failed to turn up a single major religion looking to join forces with Crackedism, the official religion we promised to make up, one of the publishers said something that made us realize that life's "big questions" had changed.

"Life's big questions have changed," she said. "Why don't you write a book called *You Might Be a Zombie?*"

Whether she realized it or not, that lady (whose name now escapes us) had given us the idea for our book. Nobody needs to know the meaning of things like existence and words anymore. Hollywood has already answered those questions for us. Modern people have more-pressing concerns, like "Seriously, I've been sprinting for like ten minutes straight. Why won't this enormous hornet stop chasing me?" and "Did . . . did it just shoot poison at my eyes?"

The answers to those questions and more are contained somewhere in the following pages. We don't want to spoil it for you, but the short answer to the second one is yes, that giant hornet did just shoot poison at your eyes. That shit happens *all the time*.

DIRECTIONS FOR PROPER USE

You Might Be a Zombie should be read in a seated position.

Due to risks posed by rapidly descending jaws, males are advised to wear an athletic supporter.

Females are advised to wear as little as possible, though that's more of a marketing thing.

INTRODUCTION

During the course of reading, you may find yourself mo-
tivated to lead a torch-wielding mob to the home of every
teacher who failed to tell you about Teddy Roosevelt's life.
Our legal department asks that you resist this impulse or, at
the very least, that you blame it on *Catcher in the Rye*.

SHOCKING BUT UTTERLY TRUE FACTS!

Jordan Monsell

THE FIVE MOST HORRIFYING BUGS IN THE WORLD

THERE are about 10,000,000,000,000,000,000 insects on earth at any given moment. Seriously, that's a real number. For every one of us, there are 1.5 billion bugs.

But some of them are so horrifying, just one is too many. Here are five you'll want to avoid at all costs.

5. JAPANESE GIANT HORNET
(*VESPA MANDARINIA JAPONICA*)

It's the size of your thumb, and it can spray flesh-melting poison. We really wish we were making that up for dramatic effect because, goddamn, what a terrible thing a three-inch, acid-shooting hornet would be, you know? Oh, hey, did we mention it shoots the acid directly into your eyes? Or that the poison also has a pheromone cocktail in it that'll call every hornet in the hive to come over and sting you until you are no longer alive?

Also, it can fly fifty miles in a day. It'd be nice to say something reassuring at this point, like "Don't worry, they only live on top of really tall mountains where nobody wants to live," but no, they live all over the freaking place. They kill more people in Japan than all animals—venomous, nonvenomous, irradiated mutant—combined. At least forty people die that way every year, each of them horribly.

You'd think the fact that humans aren't their favorite target would provide some measure of consolation. You'd think that until you heard what they do to bees. An adult hornet will fly miles to pick a fight with a hive humming with thousands of them. Outnumbered, the *Vespa mandarinia* sprays the nest with some of the acid/pheromone and brings in reinforcements, usually thirty or so fellow hornets. They then descend upon the beehive like an unholy plague of hell-born death engines and proceed to make this world a scary place.

In three hours, thousands of adult bees will be lying around, in piles of limbs and heads and bits of things that could possibly have been alive at one point, and the hornets will have stormed the hive and flown away with all the bee's children, who will then be eaten.

Yeah, nature is hard-core.

4. BULLET ANT (PARAPONERA CLAVATA)

It's a full inch long, lives in trees, and can and will fall on you to scare you away from its hive—the one you didn't know was there, because it's in a goddamn tree. Before it does this, it shrieks at you. This ant, you see, can shriek.

It's called a bullet ant because its unusually severe sting feels like you're getting shot. On the Schmidt Sting Pain Index (yes, somebody with the worst job in the world has calibrated the relative pain of different insect stings), bullet ants rate as the number one most try-not-to-shit-out-your-spine painful in the entirety of the phylum Arthropoda.

Also—and we do feel the need to stress this—they f**king shriek at you before they attack.

Some of the peoples indigenous to the Central American rain forests, where bullet ants live, use them as part of their initiation-to-manhood ceremony. You know the kind. In the West it's a big party where your relatives give you money. In bullet ant country, they knock out a few hundred bullet ants with naturally occurring chloroform, weave them into leaf sleeves so their heads are stuck and their stingers are facing inward. They then wait for the ants to wake up cranky, put the sleeves on their arms, and immediately have the holy bejesus stung out of them by—and this is important—the hundreds of bullet ants woven into the sleeves, stingers inward. The goal is to leave them on for ten minutes, after which the young man's arms are stiff, useless lengths of twisting agony, and his body wracked with uncontrollable spasms for days. In order to actually become a man, they have to endure this ritual twenty times.

3. AFRICANIZED HONEYBEE
(APIS MELLIFERA SCUTELLATA)

You know how you can spot one of these? You can't. There is no physical way to determine the difference between an Africanized bee and a common European bee.

You can, however, easily tell the difference based on their behavior. Regular bees will give you about nine seconds of being too close to their hive before attacking you. They'll typically consider you chased off after about three hundred feet.

Africanized bees do not roll like that. They give you half a second of being too close before they decide it is time to completely mess your shit up. They empty the entire hive—tens, maybe hundreds of thousands of angry, angry bees. When you run, flailing and crying and soiling yourself screaming, "Jesus Christ, I'm covered in bees!" they will chase you for over half a mile.

Africanized bees owe their existence to science. Warwick E. Kerr created them in Brazil during the 1950s by crossing a European bee with an African bee. He wanted a bee that could live in the jungle. He got a bee that swarms by the hundreds of millions, is insanely territorial and mindlessly aggressive, has already killed more people than European honeybees in a relatively brief time in existence—and can live in the jungle.

2. ARMY OR SOLDIER ANT
(ECITON BURCHELLII)

By now, you will not be surprised to hear that these ants are huge, with the soldiers reaching a half inch in length. You will also not be surprised to learn that they have massive, powerful, machete-like jaws half the length of the soldiers themselves.

They're notorious for dismantling any living thing in their path, regardless of size. They're also completely blind, which for some reason makes the whole thing worse.

They're called army ants because the entire colony, comprising up to and over one million insects, is a 100 percent mobile battalion. They don't make permanent hives, like other ants; they bivouac down in single locations just long enough for the queen to push out thousands of eggs, while the soldiers spread out in wide fans in search of food. Then the eggs hatch and they enter the dreaded swarm phase of their existence.

Jordan Monsell

Much like the word *killer*, nature takes words like *dreaded* and *swarm* very, very seriously. The ants go on the move, a near-solid mass of insect death and horror, moving steadily and swiftly along the jungle floor, flaying alive and disassembling every living thing too stupid, slow, or asleep to get out of the way. There are no painful stingers or ballistic acids; this is the kind of terror that simply flows over you by the hundreds of thousands and rips you apart with unbelievably powerful jaws, utterly and literally blind to size and species, considering everything in its path to be a threat to the continuation of the colony.

There are reports of animals the size of horses being overwhelmed and shredded by them. Go stand next to a horse and then think about what that means for you.

Army ants are also masters of wholly organic, living architecture. For the good of the colony, the ants will use their own living bodies to build any conceivable structure necessary, latching on to each other to create protective walls and ceilings against the ravages of the weather, bridges to cross otherwise impassable spans, whatever happens to be needed.

There is no other living thing in the entire world that does this.

And, they're blind.

1. BOTFLY

Oh boy. Ohhhhh boy. Okay, botflies.

Each variety of botfly is highly adapted to target a specific animal, and they have delightfully descriptive names like horse stomach botfly, sheep nose botfly, and, hey, guess what? Human botfly. The details vary, but each botfly has the same MO.

The horse stomach botflies, for example, lay their eggs in grass. Horses eat the eggs when eating the grass. The eggs hatch in the heat of the horse's mouth; then the larvae chew through the horse's tongue and burrow into its belly. There they meet up and dig honeycombs into the horse's stomach, getting fat. When they're ready to be flies, they just let go and get pooped out of the system.

The human botfly lays its eggs on a horsefly or a mosquito, which finds a human and lands on him or her. The eggs rub off onto the human, whose body heat hatches them. The larvae drop onto the skin and burrow right the hell in. Where they live. Under your skin. Eating.

The larvae can grow anywhere in your body; it just depends on where the eggs wind up. You could end up having a fat wormy thing in your tear duct. Or eating through your brain. We know, because it's happened.

Anthony Clark

THREE COLORS YOU DON'T REALIZE ARE CONTROLLING YOUR MIND

"COLOR doesn't matter; it's what's inside that counts." "Love is color-blind." "There's no black and white; everything is just shades of gray." Phrases like these dismiss the influence of color, but that's not what science says: Science thinks colors are screwing with your head pretty much 24-7.

3. BLUE

Blue skies signal a nice, relaxing day, and blue eyes have more songs written about them than all other eye colors combined. People who don't fish or swim will pay more money to live next to the ocean blue. It seems that blue just happens to be associated with a lot of the things that make us feel good about the general state of the world.

Well, actually, science says it might not be a coincidence that all those blue things make us feel so damn good. After all, blue is the only color in the spectrum that has actively prevented people from killing themselves.

Wait, what?

Blue has a scientifically proven calming effect on human emotion, and that's being exploited in a variety of ways. In 2000, police in Glasgow, Scotland, installed blue streetlights in high-crime areas. Since then, crime in those notoriously dangerous neighborhoods has dropped by 9 percent.

Figuring anything that might reduce drive-by head butts in the heart of *Braveheart* country was worth a try, police in England and parts of Japan began using the color blue around popular suicide destinations like Blackfriars Bridge in London, which was repainted blue in an attempt to reduce the number of jumpers. For the same reason, several large Japanese railway companies switched exclusively to blue light at all their railroad crossings. So far it's been an astounding success: In 2007, the year before the lights were installed, there were 640 suicides by train. In 2008, after the switch was made, there were none. Zero!

If you find yourself asking the perfectly valid question, "What the hell?" hold on: It gets weirder from there. One theory states that the color itself has a tangible, biological effect on our brain chemistry. Harold Wohlfarth, president of the German Academy of Color Science, conducted a study that found the color of lighting did indeed have an effect on children, but even more bizarrely, it had an equal effect *even if they were blind*.

It's hard to argue that children have preconceived notions associated with a color when you have to stop in midsentence and explain the entire *concept* of color to them until they break down and cry about all the things they're missing. Wohlfarth believes that traces of the electromagnetic energy that makes up colored light affect certain neurotransmitters in our brains. When light of a certain color falls on an eye, even if it's the defective nonseeing variety, it's relayed to the gland that produces melatonin, which sets off a chain reaction that elevates mood and calms emotions. Basically: blue gives you eye orgasms.

2. RED

It's what you "paint the town" if you're about to go out and get drunk (assuming you drink with your grandpa). It's the color that tells bulls to charge, that tells people to stop (assuming they're not suicidal and approaching a Japanese train track). It's what mysterious women wore in 1980s soft-rock ballads, a decade when it was generally assumed that painting your car red would make it go faster. Yes, people have believed and said a lot of contradictory, ridiculous things about red over the years, and they can all be backed up by science.

Winston Rowntree

Wait, what?

Behavioral studies have revealed that the color red leads to heightened respiratory and cardiovascular rates. This encourages a sense of heightened awareness, making people more likely to act on impulses and therefore more aggressive.

That's why red is a common color in bars and restaurants. An experiment on partygoers was conducted by a group of designers and architects, who specially built model rooms decorated entirely in solid colors. They found that the red room was by far the most popular with revelers, who not only flocked to that room in greater numbers but also left substantially earlier. "But why would they leave early?" you might ask if you've never had irresponsible, drunken sex with a stranger. It's the same reason why "red-light district" isn't just a name—where you find brothels, you will usually find red lights bathing the street in the international color of bad decisions.

But if red makes us worse at controlling our impulses, why do we use it on stop signs? Well, as coffee drinkers know, having elevated heart and breathing rates helps people pay attention. In a study conducted by the University of British Columbia, red was proven to focus attention and increase performance in detail-oriented tasks.

But the stimulant red seems most closely related to is cocaine. Like that drug, red speeds up your pulse, heightens your awareness, and was integrally involved in making the eighties an embarrassing decade to live in. Only, red is still getting you high every day of your life, whether you know it or not.

1. PINK

So all those connotations of femininity—of passivity and gentleness—that's all a lie, right? Wearing pink is just a way of expressing how comfortable you are with your masculinity, right? Not so fast: turns out pink may actually be girlier than you ever imagined.

Wait, what?

Back in the day, high school football teams would often paint the visiting team's locker room pink. The gesture was probably given as much thought as whether to call the opposing kicker Nancy or Sally, but then it began to show serious results. Teams that did it won. A lot. So much so that the University of Hawaii and University of Colorado adopted this practice in the NCAA. Unbeknownst to visiting players, the walls didn't just mock their sexuality but actually sapped their will to fight: Overwhelming win-to-loss ratios were recorded by home teams whose visiting locker rooms were painted pink. It was so effective, the NCAA's Western Athletic Conference banned the pink visitor's locker room like it was a performance-enhancing drug.

Operating on the same logic, the sheriff's office in Mason County, Texas, converted all its inmates' uniforms to pink, including shoes, socks, and even underwear (which brings up an important, if slightly tangential, question: There's jail-appointed underwear?). The chief goal of this practice, according to the sheriff, was to reduce theft. And it worked. Not only did theft rates drop to zero after the switch, but overall repeat-offender imprisonment rates are down 68 percent as well.

Pink is such an effective calming influence that a specific shade, called Baker-Miller pink, currently graces the walls of many drunk tanks and solitary confinement cells across the country. One such facility is the U.S. Naval Correctional Center in Seattle, Washington. Before switching its color palette, it averaged one assault on staff every day. After going pink, there was none for six months. So either pink is subliminally pacifying violent criminals across the world, or the secret motivation for all crime is the desire to be pretty, and having satisfied it, these hardened criminals are simply and finally happy.

Dr. Alexander Schauss, director for the American Institute for Biosocial Research in Tacoma, Washington, has suggested that pink also has neurological effects on physical abilities. Even if a person wanted to be angry or aggressive, their body would be less likely to respond in the presence of pink. Somehow it limits their heart rates and makes the adrenaline surge needed for most violent actions nearly impossible.

Of course, wearing pink doesn't necessarily mean that *you* are affected by it. After all, if it's on your body you're less likely to see it yourself. But everybody else? Well, they have to see it every time they look at you. Do you realize what that means? Wearing pink doesn't make you a wimp; it makes *everybody around you a wimp*. Technically speaking, that means the toughest guy in *any* given situation is the guy in the My Little Pony shirt.

Anthony Clark

THE FOUR MOST BADASS PRESIDENTS OF ALL TIME

THE stories you learned in school about some of America's most important presidents skipped a few details. Most of what you know about the guys whose faces are on the money in your pocket and the mountain in North Dakota were edited for the same reason health class edited out the best aspects of human sexuality: Because telling you the truth was far more likely to end with you putting someone's eye out.

4. ANDREW JACKSON

When the 1828 election rolled around, a lot of people were terrified when they heard Andrew "Old Hickory" Jackson was running. If you're wondering how a guy we're calling a badass got such a lame nickname, it's because he used to carry a hickory cane around and beat people senseless with it, and if you're wondering why he did that, it's because he was a freaking lunatic.

Former Democratic senator and secretary of the treasury Albert Gallatin feared a Jackson presidency because of the man's "habitual disregard of laws and constitutional provisions." In other words, the guy was a loose canon—nineteenth-century Washington's answer to Martin Riggs. Sure, he probably didn't have an irate black lieutenant to answer to, or a weary partner who was too old for this shit, but he most certainly had a death wish.

How do we know? Despite everyone's best efforts, Jackson was elected to the top office, and when he wasn't busy shaping the presidency as we know it today, you could find him out back dueling. In case you haven't been to the nineteenth century lately, this unmanly sounding activity involves standing across from an armed man and shooting at him while he in turn shoots at you. The number of duels that Jackson took part in varies depending on which source you consult: Some say thirteen, while others rank the number somewhere in the hundreds, either of which is entirely too many times for a reasonable human being to stand in front of someone who is trying to kill them with a loaded gun.

On one occasion, Jackson challenged a man named Charles Dickinson to a duel (the reason behind it wasn't important, not to us and certainly not to Jackson), and Jackson even politely volunteered to be shot at first. Dickinson happily obliged and shot Jackson, who proceeded to shake it off like it was a bee sting. When Jackson returned the favor, Dickinson was not so lucky, and that's why his face isn't on the twenty. The bullet, by the by, remained in Jackson's body for nineteen years because he knew that time spent removing the bullets would fall under the category of "time not dueling"—Jackson's least favorite category.

Looking back on his life, spent murdering people for little to no reason, Jackson reflected, "I have only two regrets: I didn't shoot Henry Clay and I didn't hang John C. Calhoun." Calhoun, it should be noted, was Jackson's vice president.

Greatest displays of badassery: Andrew Jackson was the first president against whom an assassination attempt was made. A man named Richard Lawrence approached Jackson with two pistols, both of which, for some reason, misfired. Jackson proceeded to beat Lawrence nearly to death with his cane until aides pulled him off.

The guns were inspected afterward, and it was discovered that they were in perfect working order, leading some historians to believe that it was an odds-defying "miracle" that Jackson survived. But we're pretty sure the bullets, like everyone else, were simply scared of Jackson.

3. JOHN F. KENNEDY

Nowadays, John F. Kennedy is remembered mostly for getting shot in the head, which, while admittedly badass, barely makes the top ten of badass things he ever did. Plagued with a bad back his entire life, Kennedy was disqualified from service in the army. Instead of using this as an excuse to pursue the decidedly saner strategy of staying away from exploding things, Kennedy had his dad pull a few strings so he could sneak his way into the navy, where he eventually became a lieutenant. Just to get some perspective, Bill Clinton dodged the draft, Grover Cleveland paid someone else to go in his place when he was drafted, but Kennedy beat the system by forcing his way *into* the navy. Once there, he handled himself like a gravel-eating shit miner instead of the rich Boston pretty boy he actually was.

Upon leaving the navy, he took up boning on a near full-time basis. Sure he dabbled at being a senator and a president or whatever, but his full-time job was pimping. While almost no two sources are in agreement as to just how much tail Kennedy snagged, historian John Richard Stephens says that "Kennedy confided with friends that he could only be satisfied with three women a day." Kennedy's closest friend once recalled that "Jack could be shameless in his sexuality . . . He would corner them at White House dinner parties and ask them to step into the next room away from the noise, where they could hold a 'serious discussion.'" Next time you're at a dinner party, go ahead and try that "Hey baby, let's go have a serious discussion" line out and then come back and tell us how much sex you didn't have.

JFK's sexual conquests allegedly include Marilyn Monroe, Audrey Hepburn, Jayne Mansfield, Angie Dickinson, Brazilian actress Florinda Bolkan, and famous burlesque stripper and rap name pioneer Blaze Starr. There are even rumors that he had sex with his insanely hot wife once in a while too.

Greatest display of badassery: In August 1943, while serving as skipper of *PT-109*, Kennedy's boat was ripped in two by the Japanese destroyer *Amagiri*. Kennedy and his crew were tossed into the water and surrounded by flames. Kennedy managed to swim four hours to safety while towing an injured crewman by the life jacket strap with his teeth. His goddamned teeth!

2. GEORGE WASHINGTON

Plenty of people know George Washington as the Father of Our Country, but few people know—and this is, perhaps, more important—just how similar he was in behavior to the Incredible Hulk.

As described by Thomas Jefferson, George Washington "was naturally irritable," and when his temper "broke its bonds, he was most tremendous in his wrath." One time, in fact, he became "much inflamed [and] got into one of those passions when he cannot command himself." Witnesses agreed that after these sudden bursts of rage, Washington generally became calm and amiable again. Sound like anyone you know? Anyone incredible, perhaps? The Iroquois Indians affectionately nicknamed Washington Caunotaucarius, which translates to something like Town Destroyer or Devourer of Villages. We were really hoping it translated to One Who (When Angry) You Will Not Like so we'd have more evidence for this whole Incredible Hulk thing, but Town Destroyer is pretty cool too, we guess.

Washington wasn't just a shirt-ripping comic book character waiting to happen, he was also an amazing general and, possibly, totally invincible. Washington was always at the front line in any of the many battles he took part in, and there are countless stories of Washington returning from battle with bullet holes in his uniform or without a horse (it having been shot out from under him), but he always remained unharmed. In a letter to his brother, he described being surrounded by bullets and death and concluded by saying, "I heard the bullets whistle and, believe me, there is something charming to the sound of bullets." When he caught news of this, George III reportedly remarked that Washington's attitude would change if he heard a few more. Washington went on to hear hundreds more and to rout King George's army in a war.

Greatest display of badassery: Making America.

1. THEODORE ROOSEVELT

Checking Teddy Roosevelt's resume is like reading a how-to guide on ass-kicking manliness. He was a cattle rancher, a deputy sheriff, an explorer, a police commissioner, assistant secretary of the navy, governor of New York, and a war hero. Out of all his jobs, hobbies, and passions, Roosevelt always had a special spot in his heart for unadulterated violence. In 1898, Roosevelt formed the First U.S. Volunteer Cavalry Regiment, known as the Rough Riders. Most people already know of the Rough Riders and their historic charge up San Juan Hill, but few know that, since their horses had to be left behind, the "riders" made this charge entirely on foot. You just could not stop this man from violencing the hell out of a San Juan Hill.

And don't think that Roosevelt lost his obsession with violence when he became president. He strolled through the White House with a pistol on his person at all times, even though, with his black belt in jujitsu and his history as a champion boxer, it wasn't like he needed it.

It wasn't just his war record or the fact that he knew several different ways to kill you that made Roosevelt such a badass. It wasn't even the fact that he decorated the White House with African lions and a bear he'd personally killed. Teddy Roosevelt was a badass of the people. Roosevelt received letters from army cavalrymen complaining about having to ride twenty-five miles a day for training and, in response, Teddy rode horseback for a hundred miles, from sunrise to sunset, at fifty-one years old, effectively rescinding anyone's right to complain about anything, ever again.

Did we mention he had asthma when growing up? He did, and after he beat asthma to death, he ate asthma's raw flesh and ran a hundred straight miles off the energy it gave him.

Greatest display of badassery: While campaigning for a third term, Roosevelt was shot by a madman and, instead of treating the wound, delivered his campaign speech with the bleeding, undressed bullet hole in his chest. At the time of Roosevelt's death, a fellow politician noted: "Death had to take him sleeping, for if Roosevelt had been awake there would have been a fight."

We have no witty commentary here. That is just straight-up badass.

Anthony Clark

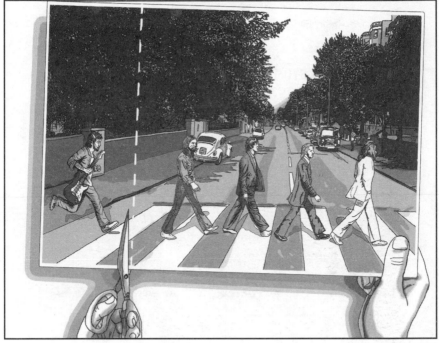

Robert Bogl

FIVE FAMOUS ARTISTS WHO DIDN'T CREATE THEIR SIGNATURE CREATION

A signature achievement is typically considered a stand-alone moment, epitomizing all that is worthwhile, unique, and memorable in one's career, or at least a defining work that sets a standard in its field. For Hemingway, it was *The Sun Also Rises*, for Stanley Kubrick it was *2001*, and for Radiohead it was *OK Computer* (Shut up! It was *OK Computer*). But what happens when—either by public misperception or private manipulation—simply too much credit is given for a signature work? Not much, actually, but it makes a tidy little list.

5. TIM BURTON DID NOT DIRECT TIM BURTON'S *THE NIGHTMARE BEFORE CHRISTMAS*

Ask anyone what their favorite Tim Burton movie is and they'll tell you *Edward Scissorhands*. But roll your eyes, and say, "Yeah, besides that," and they'll probably say *The Nightmare Before Christmas*. The stop-motion animation managed to capture Burton's quirky, dark vision and the imagination of mainstream audiences, proving once and for all that Tim Burton was no one-hit wonder as a director and that he could in fact do it in different mediums.

Well, except that it didn't do any of those things. It would have if Tim Burton had directed *Tim Burton's The Nightmare*

Shannon O'Brien

Before Christmas. While he produced it and wrote the poem it was based on, Henry Selick of *James and the Giant Peach* was tapped for the actual directorial duties.

Why didn't you know that?

When you put your name in the title of something, people just kind of make assumptions. And just like the rest of Burton's movies, it's dark and creepy, with great moments and horrible plot and pacing problems. Plus, it's unlikely you knew Henry Selick's name at the time. The studio made the rational decision to go with the name you'd heard before.

It worked out pretty well for everyone except Selick, whose name you probably still don't recognize. His biggest achievement subsequently has been directing Neil Gaiman's *Coraline.* In a cruel twist of fate, that movie was promoted as a new film from the director who brought you *The Nightmare Before Christmas,* which by then you heard as *Tim Burton's The Nightmare Before Christmas.* So the few people who did show up to Selick's failed follow-up were probably only there because they thought it was directed by Burton. Ouch.

4. GEORGE HARRISON'S GUITAR DIDN'T WEEP ON "WHILE MY GUITAR GENTLY WEEPS"

No one's denying George Harrison's talent. He wrote some of the Beatles' most famous songs while vying for album space against two of the greatest pop songwriters of all time. (If you're too young to know who we're referring to, go ask your parents, and be sure to tell them your upbringing was an abject failure.) But of all his accomplishments, George is probably best known for his classic cut "While My Guitar Gently Weeps," featuring a searing and wailing guitar solo that fully realizes the promise of the song's evocative title and that was laid down by George Harrison's best friend, Eric Clapton, and not by Harrison.

Why didn't you know that?

"While My Best Friend Eric Clapton's Guitar Gently Weeps" just didn't have the right cadence to it. The Beatles weren't touring at the time and no one was making music videos, so it's not like you could *see* George not playing the part. Also, the Beatles were never very into liner notes, which is why everyone from Clapton to Billy Preston to the old guy who repairs guitars at your town's music shop has been called the fifth Beatle at some point.

3. JOHN F. KENNEDY DID NOT WRITE PROFILES IN COURAGE

Much of Kennedy's presidency remains debated by modern historians. Some praise him as a president whose charisma and vision inspired a generation to public service and led the charge to the moon. Others claim that if you put him in a room with Marilyn Monroe, obscene amounts of pain medication, and a horribly planned Cuban invasion, Kennedy wouldn't be able to decide which one to do first. But what everyone seems to agree on is that *Profiles in Courage,* the book Kennedy won the Pulitzer Prize for, is a damn fine read. *Profiles* examined the bold decisions of eight U.S. senators and brought Kennedy the national attention and respect that was instrumental in building momentum for his presidential run.

What's not as clear is how instrumental Kennedy was in actually writing it. Although odds are good that Kennedy *read* the book, credible evidence indicates that Kennedy's speechwriter, Ted Sorenson, wrote the majority of it. In 2008, Sorenson claimed in his autobiography that he "did a first draft of most chapters," and "helped choose the words of many of its sentences." In literary circles this is known as "writing the book."

Why didn't you know that?
People tend to assume you've written something after you've won a Pulitzer Prize for it. Also, Kennedy allegedly paid Sorenson more than half the book's royalties from its first five years in print, which is probably why it took Sorenson fifty years to blow the whistle. And lastly, Kennedy was probably too busy dragging soldiers out of sinking ships with his teeth like a goddamned rescue dog and inventing a cure for headaches that nine out of ten doctors agree is a hell of a lot more fun than aspirin (see page 207).

2. BARRY MANILOW DID NOT WRITE "I WRITE THE SONGS"

Although he put together a string of pop hits in the 1970s, Barry Manilow is perhaps best known for his 1975 signature song "I Write the Songs," which topped *Billboard*'s charts for two weeks and won Manilow a Grammy for Song of the Year. In it, Manilow sings:

> I write the songs that make the whole world sing.
> I write the songs, I write the songs.

A little misleading since those words were written by Bruce Johnston of the Beach Boys. In fact, Manilow wasn't even the first person to *cover* it.

Manilow wrote a lot of his own songs, just none of the ones you've ever heard before. "Tryin' to Get the Feeling Again,"

"Weekend in New England," "Looks Like We Made It," "Can't Smile Without You," and "Ready to Take a Chance Again" were all written by other people. He did turn a cover of the UK hit "Brandy" into a U.S. hit called "Mandy," a change that probably required *some* writing, or at least the use of a pen.

It was legendary Arista Records exec Clive Davis who pushed Manilow to cover "I Write the Songs." So a more accurate chorus would be, "I sing the song that Clive Davis tells me to."

Why didn't you know that?
Quite simply, he's ugly. Most people assume Manilow was a hit-writing machine because in the looks department, he's a passable girlfriend for your bookish aunt who wears Sally Jessy Raphael glasses. At best.

1. ORSON WELLES DID NOT WRITE *CITIZEN KANE*

Citizen Kane, the fictionalized account of publisher William Randolph Hearst's life, is often referred to as the greatest film ever made. To say it's Orson Welles's signature work is an understatement. It's like the *Citizen Kane* of understatements. Film geeks speak of the film with biblical reverence, and non–film geeks know better than to question them. It's one of the great achievements in American popular art, and most assume Welles conceived and birthed it whole after a night of hermaphroditic self-love.

Which is odd, since even according to the movie credits Welles is the secondary author to screenwriting veteran Herman Mankiewicz. In fact, the few people alive who still give a shit think that Welles's contributions to the script were minimal. Rita Alexander, who took Mankiewicz's dictation for the script, was quoted as saying that Welles did not write or dictate one line of the script. Furthermore, film critic David Thomson, author of a book about the film, has said that "no one can now deny Herman Mankiewicz credit for the germ, shape, and pointed language of the screenplay."

Why didn't you know that?

Because it turns out that Welles was kind of a dick. He wanted the world to think he was a one-stop, all-purpose, filmmaking wunderkind. The RKO-produced program handed out at the movie's premiere read: "the one-man band, directing, acting, and writing." Also, in an interview that occurred while writing credit disputes were ongoing, Welles was quoted as saying, "I wrote *Citizen Kane*."

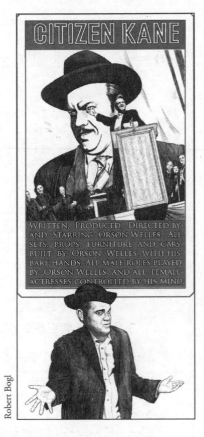

CITIZEN KANE

WRITTEN, PRODUCED, DIRECTED BY AND STARRING ORSON WELLES. ALL SETS, PROPS, FURNITURE AND CARS BUILT BY ORSON WELLES WITH HIS BARE HANDS. ALL MALE ROLES PLAYED BY ORSON WELLES AND ALL FEMALE ACTRESSES CONTROLLED BY HIS MIND.

Robert Bogl

And although Welles claimed that he intended to credit Mankiewicz all along, Mankiewicz had to complain to the Screen Writers Guild, which then insisted that Mankiewicz be given top billing. Mankiewicz also claimed that Welles offered him ten thousand dollars to let him say he wrote it all himself. So if you didn't know, it's probably because Welles wanted it that way. And for those of you keeping score, we also have it on good authority that Welles did not write his own dialogue for his appearance in *The Muppet Movie*.

Winston Rowntree

SIX TERRIFYING THINGS THEY DON'T TELL YOU ABOUT CHILDBIRTH

YOU know what's scarier than death? Birth. Anyone considering procreation should know that there are some things about childbirth they're not telling you. Disgusting, horrifying things.

6. THE CARNAGE

Many births involve a procedure called an episiotomy, which comes from the Greek word *epison*, meaning "pubic region," and the suffix *-tomy*, which apparently means "to cut the living shit out of."

In an episiotomy, a scalpel is used to artificially enlarge the vagina.

Why would the doctor want to do such a thing? Why, to keep it from tearing, of course. To the layman, this might seem like starting a knife fight to prevent a shoving match. But that's only because the layman hasn't seen the other option: Try to imagine Barney the dinosaur getting into his car by climbing in through the exhaust pipe. Well, without some controlled cutting, childbirth can be just like that but in reverse. And with blood. And instead of an exhaust pipe, it's a vagina.

Yeah, just like that.

5. THE FECES

Not even the most terrifying clips of poo porn on the Internet could prepare you for childbirth. We'll spare most of the smelly details, but rest assured that after the birth experience your view of poop will never be the same.

First off, the mom-to-be is probably going to take a rather sizable dump right in the hospital bed. Yeah, Hollywood tends to leave that part out.

Apparently, passing an eight-pound canned ham through

your hooha has a tendency to compress the intestine and push any fecal material it's holding out of the body. Thanks to a local anesthetic, Mom may not even know it happened, which means the lucky father-to-be gets to explain why the ten people in the room all just threw up in their mouths.

Secondly, the baby is gonna crap too. That isn't news. Baby shit yellow is one of the most popular colors of the new Chevy Camaro. Oddly, that same color is not an option available for the baby's first duke. For the first few days the baby's bowel movements will be black and have the consistency of fresh roofing tar—and will be approximately as easy to clean up.

To put it in perspective: Have you ever spent a night drinking cheap beer, only to wake up with a headache and a serious case of black diarrhea? It's a lot like that. Which begs the question, How did the baby get Budweiser in the womb? The answer of course is: Through the umbilical cord. Duh!

4. THE PLACENTA

Picture a vagina blowing a meat bubble. Now imagine someone surgically attaching that meat bubble to a newborn via a pulsating sausage casing.

Webster's defines the placenta as "the organ in most mammals, formed in the lining of the uterus . . . that provides for the nourishment of the fetus and the elimination of its waste products."

Urban Dictionary would probably describe it as "the lumpy, blood-soaked terror that comes out after the baby and will visit you in your nightmares for years to come."

The upside of witnessing the birth of a placenta is that the image it burns into your soul will make you thankful for the six sex-free weeks you have ahead of you. The downside is that you will forever wonder if your baby had a previously unnoticed twin who could have made you a fortune as the star of untold numbers of B horror films.

3. THE ALIEN-SHAPED HEADS

By *alien*, we don't mean the guys you picked up at the Home Depot to help deliver the baby. We mean the Sigourney Weaver–fighting kind (whose infamous chest bursting birth scene, incidentally, is the only thing most expectant fathers have to prepare them for the act of childbirth).

As it turns out, babies' heads are soft and don't become hard until months or years after they're born. This explains why you don't usually see them at college parties, crushing beer cans with their foreheads.

Either way, having a soft skull comes in handy when you're trying to be born without killing your mother in the process. Unfortunately, their heads don't instantly regain their shape once they pop out, so your offspring will spend a day or two looking like a misshapen blob of ugly before you can safely take it out in public to go hat shopping.

Winston Rowntree

2. THE FETAL MONITORING

If the doctor feels that your baby is at risk of anything (juvenile diabetes, low birth weight, high birth weight, medium birth weight), or if he just feels that he can charge you more, he may elect to hook up a fetal monitor. That doesn't sound so bad, right? Well, that's because *fetal monitor* is a nice way of saying "a twisted metal thingy with wires coming out of it that we're going to screw directly into your unborn baby's head."

Now, the fetal monitor itself isn't all that scary looking. But the fact that they jam it into the baby's soft spot while he or she is still in the womb, and leave it inside the skull until after the baby comes out, should bring back vivid memories of when that baby gets hooked up to the Matrix in the first movie.

Couple that with the fact that a baby's heart slows way down during every contraction, which sets off a little alarm on the monitor similar to the one that goes off when a patient flatlines on *Scrubs*, and you may find that you have shit your pants before the kid is even out. Don't feel bad though. Like we said, there is a lot of pooping going on at this point, so if you do let one slide, just motion toward the mother when she isn't looking and plug your nose as if to say, "Yeah, I smell it too. It was her."

1. THE BILL

Births are really expensive. Even a complication-free birth is likely to cost upward of ten thousand dollars, and if your baby comes out and so much as sneezes in the delivery room, this number is likely to start rolling up like a pinball score. Sure, maybe you're one of those fancy-pants families with "health insurance." But tack on the cost of the car seats, baby clothes, toys, diapers, bottles, playpens, and some placenta-memory-erasing Belgian ale, and you can plan on having spent the equivalent of a new car before you set foot outside the hospital.

So basically you let a strange man touch your (wife's) private parts, write him a check, watch him speed away in a Lexus, and then spend the next three months telling everyone what a miracle the whole thing was. Congratulations!

FIVE FUN THINGS
THAT WILL KILL YOU

YOU know what's fun? Fun. We spend billions of dollars a year on products and activities that serve no purpose other than distracting us from the soul-crushing daily grind for a few precious moments before we have to get back to the miserable office. But many of the things we do to lighten up the misery of our monotonous lives have the potential to end them in startling ways.

5. OWNING A SWIMMING POOL

There are approximately 7 million private swimming pools in America today, which is proof that sometimes the simplest ideas—digging a hole in your backyard and filling it with water—are the best. We'll get the obvious out of the way first: Water can drown you. An estimated 350 kids drown in backyard swimming pools every year.

Drowning in a swimming pool is the second leading cause of death in children under twelve in the United States, and, statistically speaking, having one in your backyard is more dangerous than having a gun in your house. But the danger isn't even limited to drowning: That's just the surface of the pool's lethal potential.

Jordan Monsell

(That was a wacky pun! About tragic child death!) We all had that friend in grade school who swears up and down that his friend's cousin's babysitter once knew a guy who knew a guy who got stuck on a pool's intake vent and had his guts sucked out through his anus.

That kid was so full of shit.

Except he wasn't. That's *totally true*. In 2007, CBS reported on a girl who lost her entire small intestine while swimming at her family's country club. It's rare, but anything with even one check mark in the "might tear your guts out through your asshole" column deserves to be handled with a little caution.

Studies have also demonstrated a link between chlorinated pools and cases of asthma and lung damage, and people who spend a good deal of time swimming in or working around chlorinated water are over 50 percent more likely to develop lung and kidney cancer. When you add all that together, owning a pool is like having an occupied tiger pit with a diving board attached (if tiger bites gave you cancer).

4. USING A SLIP 'N' SLIDE

What do you get when you connect one ordinary garden hose, one long sheet of plastic, and one precocious child? Well, either thirty years to life or a slip 'n' slide (depending on how the parts were assembled). The slip 'n' slide has sold over 9 million units since its inception, which is fine: slip 'n' slides are safe—provided that you are three to five feet tall and weigh less than 107 pounds. It's only when you start moving into the gray areas of "drunken adulthood" and "childhood obesity" that things start to get paralytic. See, a slip 'n' slide's thin sheet of plastic is only capable of redistributing a certain amount of weight to create that cushioning hydroplane, so heavyset kids and drunk adults trying to use it tend to hit the ground harder than Hans Gruber.

There has been a staggering number of injuries over the last fifty years from slip 'n' slide abuse, ranging from torn skin to paralysis and even death. The U.S. Consumer Product Safety Commission (CPSC) has had an ongoing investigation in place since 1993, and despite all of this, sales of the product are as strong as ever. That just proves that Darwinism is alive and well, and its official motto is, "Woo! Do a backflip!"

3. GOING TO AN AMUSEMENT PARK

According to the CPSC (which should just go ahead and change its name to the Buzz-Kill Institute of Fun Destruction), in 2008 there were about eighteen thousand injuries reported at amusement parks in the United States alone. And that's not even counting carnivals and state fairs—where you're required to undergo years of meth addiction and inbreeding before operating a ride. (To any carnies who might have been offended by that sentence: Quit making the crossing guard read to you; she has important work to do.)

Some of the injuries are just idiot comeuppance: Hundreds of people have been killed by releasing their harnesses and standing up on roller coasters, those spinning teacup rides, and Splash Mountain—not to mention one teenager who was decapitated by the Batman ride at Six Flags Over Georgia after jumping a fence to look for his hat.

That's not to say you'll survive if you follow all the safety protocols: A thirteen-year-old girl was riding on Superman: Tower of Power at Six Flags Kentucky Kingdom when a cable snapped and sliced her legs off. A man riding on the *Columbia*, a full-size replica sailing ship at Disneyland, was struck in the face by a metal cleat when a mooring line pulled it loose from the ship's hull.

There are too many moving parts to make most attractions 100 percent safe, so there's always a chance that you'll be horrifically murdered by some whirling steel monstrosity with cartoon elves painted on the side. And that's the kicker: having to tell Saint Peter, upon entrance to heaven, that your life was tragically cut short by something called the Screamin' Reamer.

2. JUMPING ON A TRAMPOLINE

Trampolines were initially conceived as a training apparatus for gymnasts. They weren't sold commercially until the 1940s, when developers George Nissen and Larry Griswold went completely insane and decided to wipe children off the face of the earth. Today about half a million trampolines are sold

Winston Rowntree

every year in the United States. Now consider that there are over two hundred thousand trampoline-related injuries annually—almost half of which result in serious emergency room visits.

Trampolines harm so many people that some personal-injury law firms have a specific telephone extension just for trampoline accidents. A twenty-year-old woman landed so awkwardly, she severed an artery and broke both bones in her leg and had to have it amputated. She trampolined her goddamn leg off! In Tasmania, a boy was jumping on a trampoline in his backyard when it turned into a remake of *Final Destination* and tossed him into a clothesline, hanging him.

There are countless safety guidelines in place to try to curb the staggering bloodlust of the trampoline. For example, it is recommended that you always jump alone and install safety nets along the edge. A boy in Colorado followed those pointers and was strangled to death by the safety netting around his trampoline. Apparently, the more you try to temper the insatiable murder frenzy of the trampoline, the more furious it becomes. In retrospect, perhaps sacrificing a few backflipping fatties a year is a small price to pay to appease its terrible appetite.

1. PLAYING ON INFLATABLE STRUCTURES

Invented by former NASA employee John Scurlock in 1959, inflatable structures (bouncy castles for readers who clap their hands when they read phrases like *bouncy castles*) are typically made out of thick vinyl and powered by motorized fans. According to the CPSC (which we're fairly certain is one lawsuit away from installing childproof locks on hugs), there have been about six thousand inflatable structure–related emergency room visits in the United States every year since 2005. You might expect injuries related to falling out and landing on the pavement, but the most *deadly* form of bouncy-castle mayhem occurs when, due to improper tethering or strong winds, the structures flip and launch people through the air like balloon-sculpture trebuchets.

An eight-year-old girl was thrown fifty meters through the air when her bouncy castle was caught by a powerful gust. In Hawaii, a girl was trapped inside a castle that got tossed into the air and flew fifty yards offshore *into the ocean!* An inflatable maze in England took flight across a field, with thirty people still stuck inside, sending two women falling out to their deaths before finally crashing back into the ground.

Perhaps the most horrible aspect of these accidents isn't the number of lives lost but the tragically inappropriate mindset of the victims right before impact. These inflatable structures are often completely enclosed, and the reason people enjoy them is the feeling of weightlessness. The poor victims often have no warning that their play structure has escaped from its tethers and is now hurtling with murderous intent toward the nearest wood chipper—they probably just think they're bouncing *really well*. Their last words are most likely, "Wheeeeee!"

COMING THIS SUMMER

BASED ON TRUE EVENTS

Anthony Clark

FIVE MOVIES BASED ON TRUE STORIES (THAT ARE COMPLETE BULLSHIT)

SOMETIMES a movie comes along and takes on special meaning because it's based on a true story, and so we watch with rapt attention knowing that real people lived through all the awesomeness on screen. But if you're going to go with the "based on a true story" tag, all we ask is that you make the stories sort of, you know, true. You can do that—right, Hollywood?

Not if these movies are any indication.

5. *A BEAUTIFUL MIND*

The Hollywood version

John Forbes Nash was really smart. When he wasn't working on the concept of governing dynamics, he was having hallucinations of Paul Bettany, seeing hidden messages in newspapers, and getting recruited by Ed Harris to break codes for the government, all while running from Russian spies. Which is even weirder when you find out all that shit happened in his head. Yep, turns out he was also really, really crazy.

The hallucinations became more frequent and, as hallucinations are prone to do, they drove him batshit insane. Fortunately, his loving wife stood by him, and Nash committed to a medication regimen, and learned to ignore his hallucinations just in time to win the 1994 Nobel Prize in Economics.

In reality . . .

There's no denying that Nash was both brilliant and afflicted with a bad case of the crazies, but filmmaker Ron Howard was widely criticized for making up the whole "seeing people who weren't really there" thing. Nash did hear voices, but that's it—his hallucinations were entirely auditory.

The love story? Nash and his wife divorced in 1963, just six years after being married. They were remarried in 2001, but it's fair to say that being married to a paranoid schizophrenic isn't the smooth ride we see in the film.

Neither is being a schizophrenic. At the end of the film,

Nash learns to ignore his imaginary friends and deliver a Nobel Prize acceptance speech dedicated to his wife. This suggests that you can reason your way out of schizophrenia, a strategy that's about as medically advisable as trying to think your way out of a heart attack. Nash would know. He quit taking his medication in 1970 and consequently has continued to be unstable, prone to shockingly unbrilliant fits of anti-Semitism.

The only thing remarkable about Nash's real Nobel Prize acceptance speech was that he wasn't allowed to give one. Public speaking opportunities are rare outside of Alabama when you're known for screaming racial slurs at imaginary Jews.

4. THE PURSUIT OF HAPPYNESS

The Hollywood version

Will Smith stars as Chris Gardner, who only wants to make enough money to provide for his adorable son. In his travels, he solves a Rubik's Cube in record time, wowing an employee at Dean Witter, and somehow (magic?) becoming a stock broker. With his son at his side, he toils for months, eventually claiming the one and only opening at Dean Witter, crying tears of joy and warming our hearts with jigginess.

In reality ...

First, while Gardner was focused on getting the job that would eventually earn him his millions, he didn't actually know where his son was. For the first four months of his program, Chris junior was living with his mother, Jackie (Linda in the movie), who refused to tell Chris where they were.

In addition, the movie tells us Gardner got arrested for unpaid parking tickets, forcing him to show up to his first day of work wearing his friend's grubby clothes. It's one of the only memorable scenes that actually happened, except instead of parking tickets, Chris was arrested after Jackie accused him of domestic violence (he claims she fell into a rose bush). That's why she wouldn't tell him where she was. During the events depicted in the movie, Chris wasn't caring for his adorable son, he was crashing on his friend Darnell's couch while the mother of his child and his son hid from him.

Don't get us wrong, Chris did indeed get his life turned around. But in the book the movie was based on, he also admitted to some things they couldn't quite bring themselves to have Will Smith do on screen. Like selling drugs or doing cocaine with Jackie (who it turns out was his mistress from a previous marriage).

Doing drugs and having sex with your mistress? Not having to worry about the resulting offspring? It says something about the man that he didn't drop the pursuit, despite having pretty much found happyness already.

3. *LEAN ON ME*

The Hollywood version

Joe Clark is badass. When Eastside High School in Paterson, New Jersey, found itself on the brink of being taken over by the state due to piss-poor test scores, Clark was brought on board as principal to right the sinking ship.

And right it he did, by fighting expelled students in the hall and throwing chains and padlocks on the doors. After all, if Joe Clark was going to go out in a blaze of glory he was going to take as many students with him as possible. In the end, thanks to a hip new school song and the bullying ways of Principal Clark, Eastside saw a meteoric rise in its test scores, and everyone celebrated by joining together in song, as inner-city ruffians often do.

In reality . . .

Apart from the fact that the test scores never improved, or that state takeover had never actually been threatened, or the various ways they fudged facts to make it appear that Joe Clark was a super badass, it's pretty close to the real story. That is to say, a man named Joe Clark did serve as principal at Eastside High for a short time in the eighties.

Here's the punch line to the whole thing: One year after Clark resigned and less than two years after the film's release, the state came and took control of the school. And since they weren't actually threatening takeover in the first place, we're forced to assume they got the idea from the movie.

2. *RUDY*

The Hollywood version

Back in the seventies, there was a plucky little football player who dreamed of nothing other than playing for Notre Dame. Unfortunately for Rudy, he was small enough to be played by Samwise from the *Lord of the Rings* trilogy, and his support system consisted of people who repeatedly went out of their way to let him know that dreams are the main ingredient in the devil's pudding.

After graduating from high school, Rudy and his best friend resign themselves to a life spent laboring in the same factory as Rudy's father and brothers. Luckily, his best friend gets blown up right in front of him, teaching Rudy a valuable lesson about how much hard manual labor sucks and reigniting his childhood dream of playing at Notre Dame. And play he does, no thanks to the evil scheming of head coach Dan Devine, who only allowed Rudy on the field after the entire team threatened to walk out otherwise.

In reality...
The real-life Dan Devine was actually the one who insisted on playing Rudy in his final game; they were good friends. Sounds like one helluva guy, right? So naturally he was repaid for his kindnesses by being turned into the Snidely Whiplash of college football in the film.

By the way, ever wonder who saw Rudy play that day and got so inspired that they just had to make the humble young factory worker's story into a movie? Nobody. Rudy himself spent a full decade trying to convince studios that his life deserved a movie before one of them finally relented. That's the spirit, little guy!

1. *THE HURRICANE*

The Hollywood version
The Hurricane is the story of Rubin "Hurricane" Carter, a boxer boasting great talent and a badass Bob Dylan song he inspired. The movie tells us how Hurricane was a promising middleweight who was falsely accused and convicted of a triple homicide, derailing his boxing career but making him prime to be the subject of a great protest song.

Luckily, after twenty years in prison as an innocent man convicted by a bitterly racist system, a few people took up his cause and, after discovering a key piece of evidence, proved Hurricane's innocence!

In reality...

First, there's a scene in the film where Carter beats the shit out of an inferior white boxer, Joey Giardello, only to lose when racist judges award the fight to the white man. In real life, Carter lost the fight so badly that the real Giardello sued the filmmakers and got a nice settlement out of it.

Now the murder thing. We're not saying Carter committed the crime, but we'll just point out that by the age of fourteen he'd already been arrested for assault and armed robbery. By twenty-two, he'd been imprisoned twice for "brutal street muggings." He was booted from the military after being court-martialed four times. But that doesn't mean he killed anyone, right?

When it came to the murders, there was enough evidence to convict him twice. Carter failed a lie detector test and at his second trial, several witnesses who had provided Carter's alibi admitted they had been asked to lie for him.

But what about that evidence that proved his innocence? There was none. The judge was forced to throw out the convic-

The Hollywood fact-checking process.

tion because the prosecution failed to turn over some evidence and thus didn't give Carter a fair trial. The prosecution could have chosen to retry the case from scratch, but they decided it wasn't worth doing since twenty-two years had passed and all the people involved were either dead or ridiculously old.

Of course the law is the law, and the law said Carter could go free. But it's probably not quite accurate to use Carter's story as proof that the criminal justice system is run by the Klan. The whole thing has really made us question Bob Dylan's research skills.

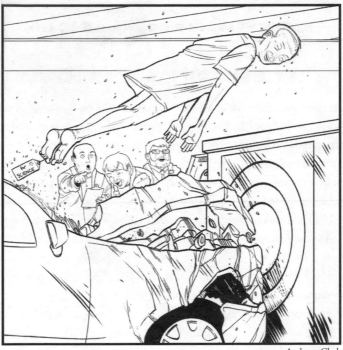

Anthony Clark

OH THE PLACES YOU'LL GO (WHEN YOU'RE DEAD): SIX INSANE THINGS SCIENCE MIGHT DO WITH YOUR CADAVER

CHRISTIANITY, Islam, Jediism—many of the world's great religions teach that the soul lives on forever. But what about the rotting hunk of Schlitz-cured blubber your soul leaves behind? If you leave your body to science, you and your soul might find yourselves watching jealously from the other side as your meat suitcase gets to . . .

6. LAUNCH HEADFIRST THROUGH A WINDSHIELD

Regardless of how kick-ass it looks in super slow motion, head butting a windshield at eighty miles per hour is generally a poor idea when you're alive. "But why would anyone want to be filmed flying into a windshield?" you might ask, if you're a nerd. The answer is simple, and also largely explains the teenage smoking epidemic: Brad Pitt made it look awesome in *Fight Club*.

The National Highway Traffic Safety Administration (NHTSA) will be more than happy to toss your stiff corpse into a car, drop a cinder block on the gas pedal, and send you flying into a ditch. In fact, the NHTSA and other agencies routinely use cadavers as crash test dummies, closely studying the carnage, frame by frame, to extract valuable insights about vehicle safety and, presumably, the occasional belly laugh.

If you *are* one of the aforementioned nerds, we've got you covered too, since dying qualifies you to . . .

5. GET SHOT INTO OUTER SPACE BY NASA

All little boys dream of strapping into a captain's chair and hurtling up into space atop a puffy white fireball oddly reminiscent of Anderson Cooper's pubic mound. Unfortunately, unless you're reading this book while doing quadratic equations upside down in the deep end of a pool, NASA probably isn't all that keen on letting you pilot their multimillion-dollar spacecraft. At least not while you're alive.

However, while developing its *Orion* spacecraft, which will begin shuttling nondead astronauts to the international space station in 2015, NASA admitted to testing its landing systems on human cadavers. In fact, NASA's been using crash test zombies since at least the 1990s, when Department of Defense–

sponsored shuttle missions brought the head of a human cadaver along to test the effects of space radiation.

While NASA probably won't be changing the motto of its space camp to "You're more useful to us dead than alive," for anyone reading a book that equates space shuttle exhaust with Anderson Cooper's pubes, that's probably not far from the truth.

Matt Barrs

4. HAVE SEX IN FRONT OF MILLIONS OF PEOPLE

Back in 1994, a Polish man named Gunther von Hagens looked at the museum scene and realized something was missing. Namely, terrified, weeping children. Thus was born *Body Worlds*, an exhibit featuring corpses that had been stripped of their skin and pumped full of plastic to preserve the appearance of every internal organ and viscous fiber. Realizing he'd created an army of terrifying meat monsters, von Hagens decided to pose them in a variety of active positions to make the exhibit fun for the whole family. After 27 million spectators across the world flocked to see his cadavers posed to mimic everyday activities such as javelin throwing, in late 2009 von Hagens decided it was time to just make them bone already.

That's why, if you die at exactly the right moment and donate your body to a sufficiently shady laboratory, you could pass from this mortal plane directly into the bone zone (medical term). While critics have denounced the exhibit as an affront to God, for those of us who spent the better part of our lives lobbying to have our gift for boning honored with a museum exhibit, there is finally hope.

3. SOLVE A MURDER

Body farms are outdoor research facilities that allow scientists to monitor decomposing corpses as they bloat and waste away in the sun for months on end. Essentially, it's like summer at the Jersey Shore, except the purpose is to better inform law enforcement about the decomposition process (as opposed to nailing a half-literate hairdresser).

Body farms at the University of Tennessee, Western Carolina University, and Texas State University painstakingly chart the progress of cadavers as they decompose, providing critical information used to analyze homicide victims and helping to bring murderers to justice.

Most of us have a difficult enough time guessing who is the bad guy in a *Law & Order* episode (hint: It's the pervy guy they interview first and hastily write off). Turns out that if you want to be the next Jack McCoy, all you have to do is lie around turning into Chester Copperpot.

2. DIE (AGAIN) FOR YOUR COUNTRY

Stepping on a land mine is generally a risky proposition for the living, but the dead are free to throw caution—and their limbs—to the wind. If you've ever wanted to be turned into human chili while making a noble sacrifice for your country, just slip a note saying so into your will.

In 2004, Tulane University found itself at the center of a media firestorm when it was revealed that seven people who had entrusted their cadavers to the Tulane science department had been blown up by the army to test land mine–resistant footwear.

A Santa Clara University professor wrote that the army used cadavers from donors who had no idea they would end up in a million bloody pieces thanks to a detonated mine. So if you donate your body and Uncle Sam gets a hankering to make it rain with your insides, you probably won't have a say in the matter.

1. STAR IN A GEORGE CLOONEY MOVIE

Forget about taking acting classes or fellating midlevel studio executives—starring alongside the sexiest man in Hollywood is just one brain contusion away. That's because Tilda Swinton isn't the only pale corpse to have shared the silver screen with the star of *Michael Clayton*.

While directing Clooney in the 1999 Gulf War flick *Three Kings*, David O. Russell filmed actual bullets entering actual human innards to capture hyperrealistic visual effects. The details of how Russell obtained a body to rekill are sketchy, but one thing is clear: Some lucky bastard got the break millions would kill for, just by being dead.

Sure, catching a hot one in the spleen is a steep price to pay for a walk-on part. But, like a true celebrity, you won't feel a damn thing.

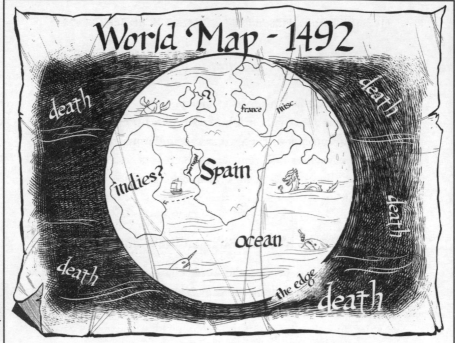

THE FIVE MOST RIDICULOUS LIES YOU WERE TAUGHT IN HISTORY CLASS

REMEMBER back in elementary school when you were at the peak of your potential as a human being? Remember all those fun stories your hungry brain absorbed about the great men who built the world around you? Yeah, that was all bullshit.

5. COLUMBUS DISCOVERED THAT THE EARTH IS ROUND

The story

In 1492, a ponce named Christopher Columbus won his long-standing feud with the Spanish monarchy to get funding for a voyage to East Asia. It had been a tough battle because everybody besides Columbus thought that the earth was a flat disc and that anyone sailing east would fall off the world's edge, presumably into the mouth of the giant turtle they thought supported it. Columbus did fail to reach his destination, but only because he crashed into the future greatest nation on earth, baby! Thus Columbus proved that the world was round, discovered America, and a national holiday was born.

The truth

In the 1400s, the flat-earth theory was taken about as seriously as it is today. Greek philosopher Pythagoras had figured out the earth was round about two thousand years before Spain even existed.

The Spanish government's reluctance to pay for Columbus's journey had nothing to do with its misconceptions about the shape of the world. Columbus himself severely underestimated the size of the earth, and everybody knew it. He eventually scraped together enough funds and supplies to get halfway to his destination, at which point he and his crew would have died horrible deaths had he not crash-landed on a continent he didn't know existed.

The myth probably began with Washington Irving's 1838 novel *The Life and Voyages of Christopher Columbus*. Elements of the fictional account started creeping into our history textbooks when editors realized that nobody wants to read history books starring some dumb asshole who lucked into inventing a country.

"What the fart?"

Anthony Clark

4. EINSTEIN FLUNKED MATH

The story
Motivational speakers love the story of a German kid who, despite his sincerest efforts, could never manage to do well in math.

That dumb ass grew up to be Albert freaking Einstein! And if he can do it, then so can you!

The truth
Actually, no you can't. As it turns out, Einstein was a mathematical prodigy. Before he turned twelve, he was already better at arithmetic and calculus than you will ever be. Not only did he pass math with flying colors, he probably could have taught the class by the end of semester.

The idea that Einstein did badly at school is thought to have originated with a 1935 *Ripley's Believe It or Not!* trivia column, which probably should have been called *Believe It or Not! I Get Paid Either Way, Assholes.* The famous trivia "expert" never cited his sources, and the various "facts" he presented throughout his career were mostly things he thought he heard, combined with stuff he pulled directly out of his ass.

According to Walter Isaacson's *Einstein: His Life and Universe*, when Einstein was first shown Ripley's supposed exposé of his early life, he allegedly laughed and politely responded that before he was fifteen he "had mastered differential and integral calculus." When he finally kicked the bucket in 1955, failure was the one concept that Albert Einstein had never managed to master.

3. NEWTON AND THE APPLE

The story

Isaac Newton was pretty much the Jesus of physics. In the late seventeenth century, he discovered the laws of motion, the visible spectrum, the speed of sound, the law of cooling, and calculus. Yes, all of calculus. Either the man was a supergenius or nobody ever thought about anything before he was born.

Probably his most famous discovery, however, is the law of gravity. The story goes that Newton was sitting under a tree one sunny day, when an apple dropped from a branch and bopped him right on the head. While most people would merely think, "Ouch! Son of a bitch!" Newton responded by formulating the entire set of universal laws governing the motion of gravitating bodies.

The truth

Newton never mentioned the thing with the apple. The first known mention of the apple thing came sixty years after it supposedly happened, when his assistant John Conduitt wrote an account of Newton's life. Even Conduitt's version is vague about whether Newton actually saw an apple or simply used it as a metaphor to illustrate the idea of gravity for people less intelligent than him (read *everybody*): "Whilst he was musing in a garden it came into his thought that the power of gravity (which brought an apple from the tree to the ground) was not limited to a certain distance from the earth."

You may also notice the account doesn't mention the apple hitting Newton in the head. That was added somewhere along the line to bring a bit of much-needed cartoonish slapstick to the history of theoretical physics.

So, why did your elementary school teachers lie? People want to believe that discoveries happen suddenly, with a light-bulb popping on over someone's head. Makes it seem like it could happen to anyone. The other option would be telling kids the truth, which makes for a much less cute story.

For example, Newton spent the best part of his life for-mulating and perfecting his theories. Hunched over piles of papers covered with clouds of tiny numbers, he put in months and years of tedious, grinding, silent, lonely work, until he had a nervous breakdown and finally died, insane from mercury poisoning. Welcome to the real world, Timmy. If you work hard enough, you too can die a lonely, broken man!

2. WASHINGTON AND THE CHERRY TREE

The story

After his father's prize cherry tree made the mistake of getting in the way of a young George Washington's ax, the future pres-ident was confronted about the crime. While a lesser founding father might have blamed a slave, Washington was unable to lie, and confessed. Thus ends the first story Americans learn about the life and times of their first president, George Wash-ington, the only superhero to ever run the country.

The truth

George Washington's elevation to the status of deity is mostly due to a man named Mason Locke Weems. He was the author of the concisely titled biography *The Life of George Washing-*

ton, with Curious Anecdotes Laudable to Himself and Exemplary to his Countrymen.

Weems recalled many fantastic stories about Washington, with particular emphasis on his overwhelming moral fortitude and infallibility. The cherry tree story is of particular importance, because it demonstrates that Washington could easily destroy things, and just chose not to.

Of course, Weems's recounting of Washington's exploits were about as historically accurate as Will Smith's 1999 Civil War documentary *Wild Wild West.*

Nevertheless, Weems's lies were taught in American school textbooks for over a century, probably because the truth—that Washington was a bullet-charming borderline lunatic—is much more likely to encourage behavior that will put an eye out (see page 208). The story still resonates today—delivered to your children's impressionable minds through such reliable media as *Sesame Street*—mostly because the central message still holds true: it's much easier to tell the truth when you're the one holding the axe

1. BENJAMIN FRANKLIN, THE KITE, AND THE THUNDERSTORM

The story

Another great American mutant superhero is Ben Franklin, the scientist and statesman whose inventions included bifocal spectacles, the urinary catheter, and freedom. But maybe his most famous experiment was the one that led to the invention of electricity.

Franklin went out into a raging thunderstorm and released a kite with a lightning rod affixed to the top and a metal key attached to the string. Annoyed at Franklin's bravery, God

Anthony Clark

Ben Franklin's typical morning ritual
(according to your sixth grade social studies teacher).

threw a bolt of lightning at him, Franklin blocked it with his
kite, the charge passed down the string and into the key, and
thus electricity was invented (somehow).

The truth

It's certainly true that Franklin at least proposed a kite experiment. It's less likely that he ever got around to performing it.
Most scientists familiar with the concepts of electricity and
kites agree that if someone flew a kite into a storm and it was
struck by lightning, they and everyone around them would be
turned into a fine mist of smoldering meat jelly.

In reality, Franklin's proposed experiment involved flying
a kite into some clouds to collect a few harmless ions, in order
to prove that the atmosphere carries a charge. The exaggerated story comes down to us by way of revisionist historian

Walt Disney and his classic cartoon *Ben and Me* (a film that also suggests Franklin's innovations are actually attributable to his pet mouse). The kite story persists to this day, presumably because anyone who's tried to replicate it hasn't survived to call bullshit.

In addition to teaching questionable lightning safety, Franklin's lightning high-five, like Newton in the apple story, portrays one of history's great geniuses experiencing naive wonder at a now-common idea, as if everyone who lived before the twentieth century was a childlike simpleton.

Why can't there be some other legend about Franklin that's closer to his real personality? Like the time he pleasured six women at once. Sure, we made that up. But if you go out and repeat it enough, it'll be in textbooks by 2050.

THE SIX CUTEST ANIMALS THAT CAN STILL DESTROY YOU

IF animals could talk, they'd spend most of their time calling us dicks and telling us to get off their land. The traits we think of as cute are often simply tricks animals have developed to get tourists to throw food. Here are six animals that you'll probably want to steer clear of, no matter how adorable they look on that wall calendar.

6. HIPPOPOTAMUS (HIPPOPOTAMUS AMPHIBIUS)

How cute!

Hippos are the very definition of Disney cute. There is no way you could look at a big, fat, squishy, huggable hippo and not think, "If she could talk like a human, she would sound just like Jada Pinkett Smith and be oh so sassy." You would totally name her Sassy-baskets, and she would be your tutu-wearing, ballet-dancing, strut-walking pal for life. Just you and Sassy-baskets against the world!

Oh shit! Run!

The next time you settle in for a game of Hungry Hungry Hippos, take a moment to reflect on the fact that hippopotamuses kill more humans per year than any other animal in Africa.

See, there's this word *territorial* that nature takes pretty seriously, especially when it's applied to a two-ton animal with teeth the size of bowling pins. It's the

Winston Rowntree

"Come on, kid. Just a little bit closer . . ."

sort of word you either pay very close attention to or ignore and end up with "Killed to death by hippo" on your tombstone.

A hippo attack usually consists of two phases. The hippo first smashes its giant head into your boat, tossing you into the water. Spencer Tyron is a good example of what happens in stage two. Tyron was hunting on an African river when, according to a 1974 *Science Digest* article, a bull hippo flipped his canoe, and then for good measure "bit off his head and shoulders."

That's probably why the late Steve Irwin, a man who used to tackle twelve-foot crocodiles for fun and wave angry snakes filled with kill-you-before-your-next-heartbeat poison at a camera, considered a five-minute sequence where his camera team had to cross a river filled with hippos to be the single most dangerous moment ever filmed on his show.

The man who *toyed with crocodiles* was scared shitless of hippos.

5. DUCK-BILLED PLATYPUS (ORNITHORHYNCHUS ANATINUS)

How cute!

We don't even know where to begin.

This is an animal so deliriously ridiculous, biologists refused to believe it could possibly be anything but an elaborate hoax when it was first discovered.

And we honestly can't blame them. There's the thick,

furry body with a flat, beaverlike tail and otterlike feet. Then there's the matter of the big leathery duck bill and the fact that they lay eggs, and it's suddenly more than a little weird, because that's . . . that's not really supposed to happen to mammals.

There are less-apparent sources of ridiculousness, like the very high degree of electroreceptivity in that bill, which helps the platypus find food buried in the silt. Like a hammerhead shark's head, only instead of being terrifying-looking eye protrusions, it's a goofy-looking duck bill. Maybe that's a little weird, as in creepy, but so? Their babies are usually referred to as platypups or puggles! *Puggles!*

Oh shit! Run!

And, they are poisonous.

Male platypuses have a pair of spurs on their hind legs that they use when dueling other male platypuses for mating rights. They deliver a brutal dose of venom that will put a human being into the emergency room and, according to an article in the *Journal of Neurophysiology*, can leave you writhing in muscle-impaired agony for months.

In other words, the platypus is Mother Nature's way of saying, "I made this thing out of spare parts I found on the workshop floor, *and it can still cripple you.*"

4. DINGO (CANIS LUPUS DINGO)

Dingo! What a silly name! It's like a Warner Bros. cartoon character or what a baby might call his penis before he knows the word.

And they're adorable. If a dingo was behind a clear plastic wall at a pet shop, we'd take him home in a heartbeat. We'd name him Bandit and put a red bandanna around his neck.

We'd take him out to the lake in a pickup truck, and he'd hang his head out the window as we drove.

If we died, he'd lie down on our graves and just howl away for the rest of his life.

Bandit would be the best dog there ever was.

Oh shit! Run!

We can practically feel you trying to reach out to give Bandit a scratch behind the ear so he knows what a good boy he's being but, seriously, *stop!*

As much as he looks like a puppy, and as silly as his name is, that is a wild, as in untamed, as in feral, meaning "thoroughly and completely a dangerous and unpredictable," animal.

Wild dogs are inquisitive, intelligent predators that travel in packs, which means there are several of them and they all think *fair fight* means "we outnumber the hell out of you." If you do a Google search for *dingo*, you'll notice the results all repeat the same sentiment ad nauseam:

Do not attempt to pet the dingo. Do not attempt to play with the dingo. *Do not let a dingo play with your infant!*

Fraser Island in Australia's population of 160 dingos has generated four hundred documented attacks on humans, killing a boy in 2001.

One other number to keep in mind when you go to pet that dingo: seven thousand. That's how many years of breeding and training it took to make your pet dog a tame and cuddly canine. This is not your pet dog.

3. CHIMPANZEE *(PAN TROGLODYTES)*

How cute!

It's that grin, that huge, toothy grin they flash for the cameras. It makes them look like devilish little scamps, like they have some great and hilarious secret they cannot wait to share. If you put a chimp in front of a camera with an action star, you have no choice but to prepare for a wild, wacky romp that will tug your heartstrings and tickle your funny bone until you vomit your entire digestive system in pure laugh-a-minute glee.

Oh shit! Run!

That is not a grin. That is a mouthful of very large teeth being bared. The chimp is attempting to inform you that you are invading his space. If you do not understand this, the chimp would be happy to elaborate—smashing his very long and extremely strong arms about your head and shoulders, grabbing your hair and slamming your head into things, all while shrieking a vicious symphony of noise that is calling all his buddies over to beat you until you cannot grow anymore. Then they pelt you with feces.

On four recorded occasions in the past fifty years, chimpanzees have abducted, killed, and eaten human babies. That's human with an *h*, as in a human baby getting wrenched out of its mother's arms, dragged off into the forest, and devoured by a chimp.

Will you please stop dressing them in cowboy outfits now?

2. SWAN (*CYGNUS OLOR* AND SEVERAL OTHER SPECIES)

How cute!

Such poise. Such grace. The way they glide effortlessly across the water. That unmistakable curve to their necks that forms a perfect heart when they nuzzle with their mates, which they will stay with for the rest of their lives.

Oh shit! Run!

Getting chased through a park by a furious bird that will not stop trying to rip the skin off your bones is only funny until it happens to you. Yes, swans are aggressive as hell. The Michigan Department of Natural Resources had to issue a swan warning in 2008 after "rogue swans" began attacking people on jet skis and motorboats. In Ireland, it is not uncommon for university rowing teams to cancel practice because there is a swan in the river. Rowing teams tend to be composed of men who are built like very large trees.

Among the useful information in the Michigan report: Swans will "fly up over and try to keep something underwater if they perceive it as a threat." Swans cannot be shooed away like mallards, preferring instead to "defend their territory forever." It's not all bad news though! Of the many swan species, the only one that hates you is the mute swan, which you'll be able to identify by its ability to sneak up on you without a sound.

Just like that girl in history class who you thought was the single most beautiful woman you'd ever seen, who you mooned over for months and left little notes for, it turns out swans are now and have always been vicious bitches who will not hesitate to snap your fingers off one by one for daring to pollute their presence before going off to laugh with all their friends about what a huge loser you are.

1. BOTTLENOSE DOLPHIN *(TURSIOPS TRUNCATUS)*

How cute!

No way. These guys save humans. Every other year or so, some diver or swimmer gets lost out at sea and these adorable creatures bring them home. Hell, in November of 2004 a bunch of these guys banded together and saved three lifeguards from a great white shark off the coast of New Zealand.

This is the only animal in the world that Americans feel proud of not eating. This is Flipper.

Oh shit! Run!

And it turns out they're sex-crazed thrill killers. How's that for a plot twist?

For the last seventeen years or so, marine biologists have been finding dead baby dolphins and porpoises washing up ashore, "mangled in unexpected ways."

The discovery that bottlenose dolphins were occasionally viciously reconfiguring their own children wasn't really all that much of a big deal. It was what the dolphins were doing to the porpoises that entered the domain of the seriously messed up.

Thirteen-foot male bottlenose dolphins were hunting down and beating porpoises to death and then playing with their corpses, all for no apparent reason. At the time of this writing, the majority opinion in the marine science community is that this breathtakingly savage interspecies homicide is for—and this is science—shits 'n' giggles.

And then there's the case of Tião, the male bottlenose that lived off the coast of São Paulo, Brazil, and was noted to be fond of humans. People flocked to the beach to swim or have their picture taken with him, until he suddenly went berserk, injuring a handful of humans and killing a grown-ass man.

Sure, some accounts say the man was drunk and was actively trying to shove a stick into the dolphin's blowhole at the time. And several locals had apparently first tried to drag it out of the water so they could take a picture with it, maybe first dressing it up with a top hat and monocle.

And here, of course, we have arrived at our lesson: When dealing with animals, you need *to forget everything you learned from cartoons*. Otherwise, the results can be deadly.

Randall Maynard

FIVE STORIES ABOUT JESUS'S CHILDHOOD THEY HAD TO CUT FROM THE BIBLE (TO AVOID AN NC-17 RATING)

THE Gospels that made it into the Bible pretty much skip from the birth of Jesus Christ to his adulthood, but there are *other* documents that chronicle the adventures of Jesus Christ: Boy Wonder. They're part of something called the New Testament Apocrypha, a series of books deemed unfit for inclusion due to concerns over the message they'd send or, in some cases, the number of faces they'd melt with their sheer awesomeness. Most of the stories are pretty normal fare—healing lepers and raising the dead—but some are so insane that we learn that the answer to, What would Jesus do? is whatever the hell he wants.

5. JESUS CHRIST: DRAGONMASTER

The New Testament didn't just descend from the skies onto newsstands the morning after Jesus ascended to heaven. The twenty-seven books in modern Christian Bibles weren't declared official until over three hundred years after Jesus walked the earth. By that time, thousands of sayings and stories about Jesus's life had to be left on the cutting-room floor. Such was the case of the Gospel of Pseudo-Matthew. The name comes from the fact that it's basically an extended director's cut of the Gospel of Matthew that made the Bible, covering most of the same territory save for one regrettably deleted scene.

Two years after Jesus was born, King Herod got word of a child being called the "king of the Jews" and ordered that all two-year-old male children in Bethlehem be killed to protect his throne (making Herod the first, and last, member of the controversial "kill all babies" political platform). But God managed to warn Joseph in time, and the family fled before Herod's men arrived. You probably knew all that. What you may not have known is that on their way to Egypt, Jesus and his family stopped to rest in a cave, which, to their surprise, was populated by a herd of dragons (what *do* you call a group of dragons? A flock? A pride? A concert?) Actual scaly, fire-breathing, winged lizard-dragons.

> And, lo, suddenly there came forth from the cave many dragons; and when the children saw them,

they cried out in great terror. Then Jesus went down from the bosom of His mother, and stood on His feet before the dragons; and they adored Jesus, and thereafter retired.

—*The Gospel of Pseudo-Matthew, chapter 18*

That's right: The Bible could have included a passage detailing how Jesus Christ *totally gave the cold shoulder to a dragon*

Jesus melts someone with his laser vision.

army. At first glance, this seems like a pretty baffling omission. Jesus Christ, dragon tamer, would have been pretty effective when converting metal heads and fourteen-year-old boys.

It makes a lot more sense if you believe that God was handling editorial duties. Jesus totally could have used his dragon-taming powers to sick an invincible hell-beast armada on Herod's ass. That's what the God from the Old Testament would have done. If *our* son squandered powers that awesome, and *we* were editing his biography, we'd probably skip that part too.

4. JESUS TAKES POOLS OF WATER VERY SERIOUSLY

Written in the early second century, around the same time most scholars date the four Gospels in the Bible, the Infancy Gospel of Thomas picks up the story a few years after the dragon taming. Back in Nazareth now, five-year-old Jesus was playing beside a small brook with some other children, forming pools of water to make clay (because fun had yet to be invented). Jesus formed some sparrows out of the clay and, since he was not the figurine-collecting type, decided to give the sculptures life, and off they flew on his command. One of the children playing with Jesus saw this and, rather than thinking, "Holy shit! That kid can create life with a word, I should probably not walk up behind him and start splashing his pools with a stick," instead walked up behind him and started splashing his pools with a stick. And Christ just goes apeshit:

> "O evil, ungodly, and foolish one, what hurt did the pools and the waters do thee? Behold, now also thou shalt be withered like a tree, and shalt not bear

leaves, neither root, nor fruit." And straightway that
lad withered up wholly.

—Infancy Gospel of Thomas, chapter 3, verses 2–3

And, like the Nazi archaeologist in *Indiana Jones and the
Last Crusade*, the boy started aging rapidly and withered away.
Sure, it would've been easier just to kill the kid, but this is
Jesus Christ we're talking about here. He's not just gonna up
and waste some kid.

3. JESUS CHRIST UP AND WASTES SOME KID

In Thomas's version of events, later that same day, as he was
casually strolling around town, running divine errands, another boy accidentally bumped into Jesus on the street. So
what *would* Jesus do? He'd probably use his divine presence to
heal the boy of being friggin' clumsy, right? Let's see:

Jesus was provoked and said unto him "Thou shalt
not finish thy course." And immediately he fell
down and died.

—Infancy Gospel of Thomas, chapter 4, verse 1

We . . . He probably . . . No. Wait. He just murdered
a kid for brushing against him? Was Jesus a Crip? Far be it
from us to question the judgment of the Son of God, but
being sentenced to death for scuffing Christ's sandals seems
excessive. Maybe if the kid had been walking exceedingly slow
right in the center of the sidewalk so he couldn't get past him
and was just obliviously yakking away on his cell phone while,
like, eight people stuck behind him were trying to get some-

where *and seriously if you would just move four inches to one side we could get past and* GODDAMN IT DON'T STOP SO THAT WE ALMOST RUN INTO YOU. OH, AND JUST TO STARE SLACK-JAWED AT A TABLOID ON THE NEWSPAPER KIOSK, YOU SON OF A BITCH—maybe *that's* a walking crime worthy of divine capital punishment. But wasting a kid because he touches your arm? Jesus was like a bully in an eighties high school movie, if they had been able to murder people with words.

2. JESUS CHRIST: SNAKE EXPLODER

By now Jesus is dominating Nazareth like Lord Humungus dominates *The Road Warrior's* wasteland. The local children feared him so intensely, they adopted him as their king and acted as his bodyguards—forcing everyone who passed through town to come and worship him. One day a group of men came by carrying a small child, and they refused to follow a group of terrified children just for the honor of worshipping their bully king. Jesus catches wind of this and asks exactly what it is they're doing that's so important they can't reserve some time for random child worship. They explain that the boy they're carrying was bitten by a snake and is near death, and would he mind it terribly if he took his boot off of their necks because they're so, so sorry? Jesus Christ (more sci-fi warlord than beacon of forgiveness in this version of the Bible), says simply, "Let us go and kill that serpent," and storms off into the woods to do what he does best: extravagant murder.

> Then the Lord Jesus calling the serpent, it presently
> came forth and submitted to him; to whom he said,
> "Go and suck out all the poison which thou hast

76

FIVE STORIES ABOUT JESUS'S CHILDHOOD

infused into that boy"; so the serpent crept to the boy, and took away all its poison again. Then the Lord Jesus cursed the serpent so that it immediately burst asunder, and died.

—*First Gospel of Infancy, chapter 18, verses 13–16*

Even *after* he acquiesces to Jesus's demands, the snake is still blown to crap by the power of God for doing what's in its nature? *Holy shit!*

1. AND THEN JESUS SAID UNTO THEM: SNITCHES GET STITCHES

By now the parents of Nazareth were understandably upset: Jesus was walking around town ruining little kids like a bad divorce. So they gave Joseph an ultimatum: Either Jesus learns to use his powers for good, or the family has to leave town. Considering that, by this point, Jesus has killed more kids than a Willy Wonka tour group, that sounded pretty reasonable. But Christ ain't tolerating no narcs up in yore:

> Jesus said, "I know that these thy words are not thine: nevertheless for thy sake I will hold my peace: but they shall bear their punishment." And straightway they that accused him were smitten with blindness.

—*Infancy Gospel of Thomas, chapter 5, verse 1*

And that was the last straw: Joseph finally decided to discipline his son. But what do you do in response to a list of crimes more befitting a Grand Theft Auto sequel than a holy child? Grounding? Caning? Imprisonment?

None of the above.

Joseph "grabbed [Jesus's] ear" and "wrung it til it was sore." You may laugh, but in the end Jesus *does* end up uncursing everybody; just not out of some well-deserved sense of remorse or the slightest hint of empathy or anything. Eventually, a local teacher starts frantically screaming to everybody that Jesus Christ is probably God, after a *Good Will Hunting*–style display of intelligence at his Nazareth grade school (funny, you'd think the boy's ability to kill with words would have clued everyone in sooner).

So now that the secret's out (the kid laying siege to entire countries with his superpowers is—surprise—extraordinary), Jesus figures he may as well reverse all the death and destruction because, hey, once you get your propers, there's just no reason to blast them bitches no more.

If you take one thing away from this, let it be that Jesus Christ wasn't born the Gandhi-like paragon of peace you know him as—he's more like a reformed con: sick of the game because he lived it too hard, for too long.

If there are two things that you take away from this, let the second be that the power of Christ is *terrifying*. Sure, miracles like bread splitting or wine making might seem a bit dull, but that's just because the Church decided that the part where Jesus became the snake-melting dragonmaster was a little too terrifying for *your* delicate sensibilities. You straight up can't handle that much Jesus.

"*Come on, honey. If you behave yourself,*
you can have some mouse fetus for the ride home."

Jordan Monsell

THE SIX MOST TERRIFYING
FOODS IN THE WORLD

LOOKING to vomit right now but lack the proper motivation? Don't worry, we got you covered. Here are six dishes that seem to have sprung from Satan's own cookbook.

6. BABY MICE WINE

From: Korea

What the hell is it?
What better way to wash down some spicy Korean food than with a nice chilled cup of dead mice babies?

Baby mice wine is a traditional Chinese and Korean "health tonic," which apparently tastes like raw gasoline. Little mice, eyes still closed, are plucked from the embrace of their loving mothers and stuffed (while still alive) into a bottle of rice wine. They are left to ferment while their parents wring their tiny mouse paws in despair, tears dropping sadly from the tips of their whiskers.

Wait, it gets worse...
Do you wince at the thought of swallowing a tequila worm? Imagine how you'd feel waking up next to an empty bottle of baby mice wine. Whoops, I swallowed a dead mouse! Whoops, there goes another one! Whoops, I just puked my entire body out of my nose!

Danger of this turning up in America
Slim. Who are you going to find in America who's OK with drinking dead baby anything with a heartbeat just because they think it might make their life just a tiny bit longer? OK, other than lawyers?

5. CASU MARZU

From: Sardinia, Italy

What the hell is it?
This, dear reader, is a medium-size lump of sheep's milk cheese that has been deliberately infested by a *Piophila casei*, commonly known as the cheese fly. The result is a maggot-ridden, weeping stink bomb in an advanced state of decomposition.

The cheese fly's translucent larvae are able to jump about

six inches into the air, making this the only cheese that requires you wear eye protection while eating it. The taste is strong enough to burn the tongue and, presumably, to melt the inside of a toilet bowl later on.

The larvae themselves pass through the stomach undigested, sometimes surviving long enough to breed in the intestine, where they attempt to bore through the walls, causing vomiting and bloody diarrhea.

Wait, it gets worse...

This cheese is a delicacy in Sardinia, where it is illegal. Yep. It is illegal in the only place where people actually want to eat it. If this does not communicate a very clear message, perhaps the larvae will, as they leap desperately toward your face to escape the putrescent horror of the only home they have ever known. Even the cheese itself is ashamed; when prodded, it weeps an odorous liquid called *lagrima*, Italian for "tears."

Danger of this turning up in America

If the cheese companies have a lot of maggot stock in the back of their warehouses that they'd like to get rid of, why not? Self-loathing is a powerful force in this economy (see the diet section of your local supermarket).

4. ESCAMOLES

From: Mexico

What the hell is it?

Escamoles are the eggs of a giant black ant (*Liometopum apiculatum*) that makes its home in the root systems of maguey and agave plants. Collecting the eggs is a uniquely unpleasant job, since the ants are highly venomous and apparently have some sort of grudge against human orifices.

The eggs have the consistency of cottage cheese. The most popular way to eat them is in a taco with guacamole, while insane.

Wait, it gets worse ...

Escamoles have a surprisingly pleasant taste: buttery and slightly nutty. This hugely increases the chances that, while in Mexico, you could eat them without realizing you are eating a taco full of ant eggs.

Danger of this turning up in America

How well do you really know what's in that burrito? Americans have proven that they'll eat anything if you dress it up in some kind of friendly sounding, pseudo-Mexican name. Taco Bell sold a soft taco called the Gordita, which means "fat little girl" in Spanish. Call them Zesty Rancho Antcheros, and we'd all be stuffing our faces with ant eggs.

3. LUTEFISK

From: Norway

What the hell is it?

Ahhh, lutefisk. After the larvae-ridden cheese, it's a blessed relief to sample a clean, down-to-earth Scandinavian recipe.

A little too clean.

Lutefisk is a traditional Norwegian dish featuring cod that has been steeped for many days in a solution of lye, until its flesh is caustic enough to dissolve silver cutlery.

Wait, it gets worse...

For those of you who don't know, lye (potassium hydroxide/sodium hydroxide) is a powerful industrial chemical used for cleaning drains, killing plants, debudding cow horns, powering batteries, and by Santiago "the Stewmaker" Meza Lopez, dissolving over three hundred victims of his drug cartel. Contact with lye can cause chemical burns, permanent scarring, blindness, or if you live in Norway, total deliciousness, assuming you're able to pour it onto a herring without getting any on your face.

Danger of this turning up in America

It's already here! Shit! Lutefisk is already gaining popularity in America, presumably among the underserved serial killer population looking to make sure they don't waste an ounce of their latest victim.

2. PACHA

From: Iraq

What the hell is it?

Of all the dishes, this is the one most likely to be mistaken for a threatening message from the mob. It's a sheep's head. Boiled.

Wait, it gets worse...

Pacha only reveals its terror gradually. Sure, maybe you can get around the fact that you're eating something with a face. But the more you eat it, the more bone is revealed, until you give a final burp and set your cutlery down beside a grinning ivory skull, its hollow eye sockets staring back at you with a look of grim damnation.

No wonder Iraqis keep blowing themselves up. If every evening meal was a haunting festival of death, wouldn't you?

Danger of this turning up in America

Tell people that sheep's head contains some kind of enzyme that boosts your metabolism, and it'll be everywhere.

1. BALUT

From: the Philippines

What the hell is it?

Our journey of horror reaches its destination. *Balut* are duck eggs that have been incubated, often until the fetus is all feathery and beaky, and then boiled alive. The bones give the eggs a uniquely crunchy texture.

They are enjoyed in Cambodia, the Philippines, and the fifth and seventh circles of hell. They are typically sold by street vendors at night, out of buckets of warm sand. You can spot the vendors because of their glowing red eyes and the faint, otherworldly sound of children screaming.

Wait, it gets worse...

Because you're never going to look at an egg the same way. Every time you crack open an egg after experiencing *balut*, you will be half expecting a leathery wad of bird to come flopping out into the skillet.

Balut is upsetting on about a half-dozen levels. Sure, all meat eaters know that the delicious chop used to belong to something cute and fluffy, which gamboled in the sun during the brief spring of its life. Most of the time, it's easy not to give a shit. But when you're biting into something that hasn't even had a chance to see its mother's face, it's . . . different.

Danger of this turning up in America

If you live in the vicinity of a metropolitan area with a large Filipino population, it's already here. Folks in central California can go to the Metzer Farms website and order up some "jumbo" *balut* for a dollar a pop. If marketed properly, these eggs could be a damn good motivator. When you've looked death in the face at breakfast time, what the hell else can the day throw at you?

Brian Patrick

FIVE WACKY MISUNDERSTANDINGS THAT ALMOST CAUSED A NUCLEAR HOLOCAUST

NOW that it's over, the cold war seems like a pretty anticlimactic conflict. No big public scares, no major disasters—but behind the scenes the shit was apparently hitting the fan so hard we half suspect the fan was the shit's ungrateful stepchild. It's hard to even count the many times we were within seconds of a nuclear holocaust, but we can certainly list off the five times when it was for the most retarded reasons.

5. THE CASE OF THE NUCLEAR "SUNBEAMS" VS. THE IRON-BALLED RUSSIAN

You are Stanislav Petrov, a Russian lieutenant colonel in command of your country's early warning system. You're sitting in your impenetrable bunker one evening when, *bam!* all your computers scream that America just went nuclear on you. Every protocol and years of training demand that in the event of a verifiable missile launch the commander in charge has to launch a counterattack.

A lesser man might've panicked, picked up the phone, and screamed, *"F**k America with missiles!"* but Petrov and his cast-iron balls had other ideas.

Jordan Monsell

How come we're still alive?

Petrov had a "gut feeling" that the alert was a computer error and ordered the counterattack delayed. As he waited, more missiles appeared, enough to trigger an automatic alert to control. Headquarters called and begged Petrov to launch the counterstrike. He refused and simply waited as the blips came closer. Because you're not reading this etched on the skin of a supermutant, you can probably guess the outcome: Petrov was right. It turns out that early warning satellites had mistaken glare from the sun for missile exhaust plumes. Thanks to the hunch of one Russian with cojones like collapsed stars, that's all now a moot point. His reward? A tiny pension, discharge, and a total cover-up. Sure that sounds shitty now, but keep in mind that back then Russians had to stand in line for four hours just for a kick in the junk; Petrov probably came away feeling whatever the Soviet equivalent of happy was. Unctuous?

4. THE CASE OF THE TEST SWITCH AND THE MISSING JIMMY

Aside from the ever-looming specter of nuclear holocaust, being an operator at NORAD was like any other boring security job. But November 9, 1979, was a bad day for the NORAD office. You know the kind—starts when somebody drinks the last of the coffee without starting a new pot and ends when the nuclear-death sirens go off, the shit-your-pants lights flash, and your boss panics so hard he completely forgets how radiation works and barricades the doors to "keep out the atoms, for Christ's sake!"

On November 9, the computers at NORAD suddenly began to register dozens of incoming missiles. The attack was taken so seriously that the White House launched the Doomsday Plane (the 747 that serves as the pentagon's mobile office in case of attack) *without* President Carter on board!

How come we're still alive?
Common sense. After ten minutes of hand-wringing, someone finally had the idea to check the raw data coming straight from the satellites themselves. Sure enough, no missiles showed up. The strange part was that these fictional missiles

weren't just the random blips typically associated with computer failure, they were *perfectly organized*, like textbook tactical . . . And that's when it dawned on them: Some idiot from the previous shift loaded a "simulated attack" training tape into the computers and forgot to set the switch to "test." The result was a terrifying missile scare at every Minuteman silo in the nation, the United States coming within moments of a nuclear strike, and Jimmy Carter's sad realization that when shit really goes down, he gets left behind harder than the kid in *Home Alone*.

3. THE CASE OF THE BROKEN NUCLEAR ANSWERING MACHINE

During the cold war, the most likely source of an American first strike against Russia was a submarine in the waters near Norway, because a single nuke, detonated that far north of Soviet territory would blind the radar to the doomsday barrage launched from the continental United States. So you can forgive the Russian radar station that detected a missile launch from Norway on January 25, 1985, for getting just a smidge nukey. Things got an awful lot nukier once they saw it separate into what appeared to be several warheads, as is standard on Trident missiles. A missile from Norway would only take about ten minutes to hit Russia.

Ten minutes.

In the time it takes most of us to decide what to watch on TV, the Russians had to decide whether or not to end the entire world over a possible glitch. The operators scrambled desperately to verify the information, and it came back as accurate. When they realized they were definitely seeing a real projectile, they sent an emergency signal to President Yeltsin's "nuclear briefcase," which is like getting to third base for Armageddon.

The call went out and all forces stood at alert for the counterstrike. With only two minutes left to ground zero, the warheads suddenly dropped into the sea and disappeared.

How come we're still alive?

Unlike the other instances, this was no computer glitch—it was an actual missile . . . just not a nuclear one; it was a scientific research rocket.

NASA had organized a rocket launch to study the northern lights.

And while it might seem a bit suicidally reckless to launch a rocket from the most dangerous watch point on earth in the direction of a nuclear superpower in the midst of the cold war, it should be noted that NASA did warn everyone of their plans several weeks earlier. But what was Russia supposed to do? Write that shit down? Have you *seen* Russian writing?

How are we still alive?!

2. THE CASE OF THE NUCLEAR PLAYDATE

On November 2, 1983, a ten-day NATO war games exercise named Able Archer 83 began, and it was quite possibly the closest mankind has ever come to nuclear annihilation. That was also the year pop-metal band Europe raced up the charts with the hit single "The Final Countdown," thereby proving that the people of 1983 were both ready for, and richly deserving of, complete obliteration.

Tensions between the Soviets and the West were already at an all-time high when the operation got under way. The Russians were so certain that Reagan was planning a first strike that the KGB drew up a checklist of events they expected to precede a nuclear attack by the Americans. And then, one by one, they all started happening: Due to the invasion of Grenada, coded messages between Britain and America increased dramatically, missiles and signals units were deployed to the borders en masse, all the NATO commanders retreated to a single bunker, and a state of DEFCON 1 was announced. Then came something the Russians hadn't even bothered to put on the list: a complete simulated nuclear missile launch.

Yep. At the height of the cold war, the Western forces

Winston Rowntree

played pretend *so hard* that they even faked a complete missile launch *directly at Russia*.

We do not deserve life.

How come we're still alive?

No one knows. All of the KGB's intelligence indicated a real attack. Many believe that the only reason the Russians held off so long was President Reagan's noninvolvement in the maneuvers. The British and German leaders were both personally involved, but the Russians decided no real apocalyptic decision would be complete without Reagan's half senility. Also, they're such a notoriously passive and sober people.

1. THE CASE OF THE URSINE SUPERVILLAIN

The human race was itching to blow the hell out of itself throughout all of 1962. America was in a state of DEFCON 3, which basically means that if somebody so much as sneezes they're getting a nuclear warhead up their ass. So the Duluth Air Defense Sector direction center was naturally in a state of high alert on October 25, the night a security guard spotted a silhouette clambering over the fence. He promptly shot the figure without notice, setting off the saboteur alarm. The alert then relayed to every silo and airbase in the region, presumably advising security to keep a sharp eye out for mustachioed men in black masks and prison-style striped shirts.

Unfortunately, someone had done a piss-poor job of wiring the alarms at the Volk Field airbase in Wisconsin, so instead of the saboteur alarm, the signal set off the main klaxon. If that alarm goes off in DEFCON 3, it means the situation is absolutely not a drill and that all nuclear bombers need to be launched.

And that's exactly what happened: the pilots took their positions, the bombs were armed, the planes started taxiing down the runway, and everybody in the tower probably started boning in typical end-of-the-world fashion.

How come we're still alive?
The wheels were just about to leave the ground when somebody managed to contact Duluth with an urgent message: the "shadowy figure" trying to "sabotage the base" wasn't a spy . . . it was some asshole bear! A car was sent tearing down the run-

way and barely managed to signal the pilots before takeoff. Another few minutes, and those bombers would have been beyond contact.

One stupid, goddamn, jerk-off bear almost ended the entire civilized world.

McFly, Martin

Brown, Emett

Anthony Clark

THE SIX MOST DEPRESSING HAPPY ENDINGS IN MOVIE HISTORY

MOVIE audiences pretty much demand happy endings. Very few hit films end with the credits scrolling over dead puppies and weeping children. But sometimes Hollywood slips one past us, giving us a supposedly happy ending that is actually depressing as hell once you give it a little thought. For instance:

6. BACK TO THE FUTURE

The "happy" ending

While on a time-travel adventure, young Marty McFly helps his father become less of a wuss and meet his future wife. After returning to his own time, Marty finds that he has a cool new truck, his formerly dysfunctional family is now happy and affluent, and the school bully, Biff, has been made into an indentured servant.

Wait a minute...

Marty's family doesn't exist anymore.

Sure the people in his house look the same, but they have completely different personalities from the people he knew and loved before he hopped in the DeLorean. The utterly different direction their lives took basically gives his parents personalities as alien to him as pod people from *Invasion of the Body Snatchers*.

Not to mention the fact that every single conversation and interaction with his parents will be based on a history he has utterly no memory of. How long until they push to have Marty institutionalized, since every memory from his childhood is from some bizarre alternate reality that no one else shares?

On top of all that, while the movie wants us to cheer Biff becoming a menial laborer for the McFlys as a nice bit of karmic comeuppance, we can't help but think that it's a bad idea to give a house key to the guy who once tried to rape your wife.

But hey, at least Marty got a cool truck out of the deal.

5. RETURN OF THE JEDI

The "happy" ending

The evil emperor Palpatine hatches a plan to defeat the Rebel Alliance once and for all by giving them the location of his unfinished superweapon and detailing how to defeat it. This plan goes about as well as you would expect. Our heroes destroy the weapon and kill the Galactic Empire's two leaders with the help of some genocidal teddy bears called Ewoks.

Wait a minute ...

That epic battle at the end? That only destroyed one base and a fraction of the troops the empire had at its disposal. The Death Star was taken out, just like it was two films before, but that didn't exactly stop them last time. Sure, Vader and the emperor were both blown up, but that wouldn't destroy the empire any more than blowing up the Pentagon would dissolve the United States.

What it does create is what's known in international politics as a power vacuum. *Return of the Jedi* leaves the galaxy with fleets of star destroyers and no coherent power structure to control them. Throw in roving gangs of pissed-off troops desperate for money after their paychecks went up in flames with the Death Star, and you start to realize how bad shit's about to get.

Soon these power-hungry military officers would form factions and destroy entire planets in their brutal attempts to seize power. Eventually, Palpatine would simply be replaced by a new emperor, possibly even one competent enough to devise a plan that can't be foiled by developmentally stunted bears throwing rocks.

4. SUPERMAN RETURNS

The "happy" ending

Lex Luthor fails to kill Superman by stabbing him with kryptonite and leaving him in a shallow pool of water, and Su-

Anthony Clark

perman stops Luthor's evil plan in a thrilling action scene that consists of Superman holding stuff over his head.

Having saved the world again, Superman says good-bye to his son and flies into space.

Wait a minute...

And by "says good-bye to his son," we mean he abandons his crippled, illegitimate son for the second time.

The whole setup of *Superman Returns* centers on earth's greatest hero knocking up his girlfriend and then skipping town for five years. While he was gone, the combination of human and alien DNA resulted in the child becoming weak and sickly, with Lois mentioning that the child was failing gym class. (What kind of PE teacher fails a five-year-old for having asthma?)

So how does our hero respond when he returns and learns about his son? By breaking into the kid's bedroom, telling him "good luck with the whole outcast thing, kiddo," and leaving him alone. Again. So we're left with a kid with:

1. superpowers,
2. gross genetic defects,
3. good reason to hate Superman.

It doesn't take an evil genius to see the supervillain potential, and you know what? If he takes on Superman, we're rooting for the kid.

3. JACK

The "happy" ending
Robin Williams plays the titular character, an elementary school child trapped in the body of a middle-age man. By the film's end, Jack's formerly intolerant classmates learn to love and accept him for the horrifying genetic aberration he is.

Wait a minute...
All this just makes it even sadder that Jack won't live to see college.

There's a reason why in other "kid becomes an adult" films the transformation is brought on by some fantasy element. In *Jack*, the main character is instead said to have a rare genetic condition that causes him to age four times faster than normal.

Now, the problem with this is that it strongly resembles an actual medical condition known as progeria. And, sadly, most people afflicted by this disease don't live past age thirteen, as you'd expect for a disease that makes you age really, really fast.

Jack won't get the ending Tom Hanks got in *Big*, where he magically shrinks back into a child and gets to live out his life as the only twelve-year-old who knows how to make love to a grown woman. Jack, meanwhile, will be walking with a cane by high school. The only way he's getting laid is if he lives long enough to see the invention of Viagra.

2. THE MATRIX TRILOGY

The "happy" ending

Thanks to the triumph of human will and several baffling plot contrivances, Neo sacrifices himself and convinces the machines who are enslaving humanity to not enslave humanity quite so much.

The machines send their Colonel Sanders avatar to announce that any humans who want to be freed from the Matrix will be allowed to do so.

Wait a minute . . .

Hey, remember in the first movie where they said they don't pull adults out of the Matrix? Because finding out that every experience they ever had was false and that the real world is a frozen wasteland destroys their mind?

Well, in this new world the whole "all of society is a computer-generated hoax" thing isn't going to stay a secret for long. How do you think society would react to finding that out? How would major religions react?

Why would anyone go to work after that? How do you think starving third-world nations would regard their machine masters, knowing that their misery is purely the invention of the machines and that the Matrix could have rained food down from the sky any time it wanted?

The world would descend into utter chaos. Luckily, the

people can escape the madness anytime they want by exiting the Matrix!

Oh, wait, they can't. In the real world outside the Matrix, the one city where people could live has been devastated by the robot attack, and there is nothing close to enough housing, food, clothing, fresh water, or anything else to accommodate even a small country.

Hey, thanks for waking us up, asshole!

Anthony Clark

1. *TOY STORY 3*

The "happy" ending

Woody, Buzz, and most of our favorites from *Toy Story 1* and *2* narrowly escape a freaky daycare full of creepy, manipulative toys and dangerous, thoughtless brats. Our heroes return home and Andy, before leaving for college, donates the gang to a little girl named Bonnie, ensuring the toys a carefree future of playing with a sweet and lovable girl forever and ever!

Wait a minute...

Until Bonnie throws them away.

The toys don't age along with their human owners. Sure, Andy was kind enough to donate them to a little girl, but who *knows* what'll happen when she grows up? The best-case scenario is that Bonnie keeps them around long enough for them to watch her die of old age.

Of course, unless Bonnie suffers some sort of head trauma,

she'll be interested for another few years max. Hell, Little Bo Peep never even made it to *Toy Story 3*. It's far more likely that they'll eventually wind up at the bottom of a rotting compost heap, sandwiched between an empty pizza box and a copy of *ASS!* Magazine. At least the hellish trash incinerator we see in *Toy Story 3* offers a quick way out.

With a fate like that in store, it's no wonder 90 percent of all fiction involving sentient dolls ends with them trying to kill their owners.

Christopher Hastings

FIVE FAMOUS INVENTORS WHO STOLE THEIR BIG IDEA

LUCKILY, we slept through high school, but we've got some bad news for those of you unfortunate enough to have stayed awake: Every brilliant inventor you've ever loved is a huge thieving asshole.

5. GALILEO GALILEI

If you asked the average high schooler what Galileo's lasting contribution to science was, they would most likely reply, "The telescope," before going off to smoke some grass and listen to Bon Jovi records (hey, we were in high school once too, you know). Well, imaginary high school student, put down that Atari and prepare to have your mind blown: Galileo did not invent the telescope. (Also, if you start *Slippery When Wet* and *The Wizard of Oz* at the same time, it sort of looks like the Tin Man is lip-synching for about two seconds of "Livin' on a Prayer.")

Who actually invented it?

Lots of scientists were looking up at the stars back then, but no one was doing it quite as hard as Dutchman Hans Lippershey. In 1608, Lippershey completed construction of the first telescope and attempted to receive a patent for it but was denied.

A few countries over, when Galileo heard about Lippershey's work in 1609, he quickly built his own telescope, one that could see just a little bit farther than Lippershey's. Necessary? Not particularly. Emasculating? Oh, you betcha. While Galileo never registered a patent, the fact remains that his name is synonymous with telescopes, while Lippershey's name was quickly forgotten.

The lesson, as always, is that having an unwieldy, nonalliterative name that sounds like an STD is never good for your career.

4. ALEXANDER FLEMING

Sir Alexander Fleming is the name people think of when penicillin is brought up. There's even a charming little story that accompanies it: Fleming's father saved a little boy from drowning in Scotland, and the father of this boy vowed to fund the young Fleming's education to repay the kindness. Eventually, Fleming graduated from med school and discovered the healing nature of penicillin, which eventually saved Winston

Churchill's life when he was stricken with pneumonia. And who was the boy that Fleming's father saved? Winston goddamned Churchill.

Two things. One, Churchill wasn't treated with penicillin. Two, Fleming wasn't the guy who discovered it. Just some asshole.

Who actually discovered it?

North African tribesmen had been using penicillin for thousands of years by the time Fleming was born. Also, in 1897 Ernest Duchesne used the mold *Penicillum glaucoma* to cure typhoid in guinea pigs, which was about the stupidest waste of time in the history of science but still proof that he understood the mold's healing properties.

Other scientists at the time didn't take him seriously, due to his age and strange preoccupation with guinea pigs, so he never received a patent. He died about ten years later, from a disease that would have been completely treatable with penicillin, and he was survived by his healthy, yet totally indifferent, guinea pigs.

Even when Fleming did accidentally discover penicillin years later, he didn't think it could be used to help anyone, so he moved on. Meanwhile, scientists Howard Florey, Norman Heatley, Andrew Moyer, and Ernst Chain disagreed and worked with penicillin until they'd mastered it.

So even though Fleming wasn't the first person to discover penicillin and didn't actually believe penicillin was useful, he will forever go down in history as a penicillin-inventing, Winston Churchill–saving genius.

3. ALEXANDER GRAHAM BELL

For being the man behind the telephone, Bell sure loved deaf people. His wife was deaf, his mother was deaf, and he was even Helen Keller's favorite teacher. With this near obsession with deaf people, it's amazing that Bell found time to invent the telephone. Wait, not *amazing*. *Impossible*. That's the one.

Who actually invented it?

In 1860, an Italian named Antonio Meucci first demonstrated his working telephone (though he called it the *teletrofono*, because Italian is a ridiculous language). In 1871, he filed a temporary patent, but in 1874 he failed to send in the ten dollars necessary to renew his patent, because he was sick, poor, and Italian.

Two years later, Bell registered his telephone patent. Meucci attempted to sue, of course, but when he tried to retrieve the original sketches and plans he sent to a lab at Western Union, the records, amazingly, had disappeared. Where was Bell working at this time? The very same Western Union lab where Meucci swore he sent his original sketches.

Did Bell, given his convenient position at Western Union, destroy Meucci's records and claim the telephone as his own invention? It's difficult to say, though it has been argued fairly convincingly that, yes, of course he did. Absolutely. Most notably, by us just now. It makes sense, if you look at the facts: Bell already had a number of important inventions under his belt; it isn't unreasonable to assume that he got greedy and didn't want to see anyone else succeed. Further, who is Bell even calling? His deaf wife and mother? Bullshit.

2. ALBERT EINSTEIN

When you hear the name Einstein, you undoubtedly think, "He discovered relativity," or "He came up with that $E = mc^2$ equation," or "He was a sex maniac." Only one of those things is true. (It's the sex maniac part.)

Who actually invented it?

Henri Poincaré was the foremost expert on relativity in the late nineteenth century, having published thirty respected books and over five hundred papers on the subject, which is strange, because Einstein's famous *On the Electrodynamics of Moving Bodies*, which contains his theories on relativity, doesn't mention Poincaré once. As a matter of fact, Einstein does not reference, footnote, or cite a single goddamn source in his entire paper.

We don't want to jump to any conclusions. Maybe Einstein's paper didn't contain any sources because he was so smart he didn't need any other current physics texts. But according to Peter Galison's *Einstein's Clocks, Poincaré's Maps: Empires of Time*, Einstein and a small group of his fellow nerdlings had a group called the Olympia Academy, which would regularly gather to discuss their own works as well as the works of current scientists. The book goes on to mention specifically how Poincaré was one of the scientists who Einstein and his battalion of nerds discussed.

Shoots that whole "maybe Einstein didn't read any other papers" theory right to shit, doesn't it? It's interesting that Einstein sat studying and discussing the work of Poincaré for years, published a book that featured a theory that was startlingly similar to Poincaré's, and then didn't reference Poincaré once in his book. Wait, that isn't interesting; it's total bullshit. Good luck sexing your way out of this one, Einstein.

1. THOMAS EDISON

Edison has been described as one of the "world's most prolific inventors," with 1,093 patents to his name. You know, a guy could round up and kidnap a shitload of children and keep them forever, but would you call that guy the "world's most prolific father"? No, of course not. A "soulless monster," maybe. A "skilled thief," if you're being generous, but you wouldn't call that guy "the world's most prolific father," because those aren't his kids. He stole them. Such is the case with Thomas Edison.

Edison is celebrated in schools across the country for inventing the lightbulb, the motion picture, electricity, and a bunch of other important crap he had very little to do with, and while all of those claims are spurious, we're just going to focus on the lightbulb today (we've only got 320 pages, you understand).

Who actually invented it?
Plenty of people messed around with the idea of the lightbulb (Jean Foucault, Humphry Davy, J. W. Starr, some other guys

you'll never read about in school), but Heinrich Göbel was likely the first person to have actually created, back in 1854, a version of the lightbulb that resembled the one we have today. He tried selling it to Edison, who saw no practical use in it and refused. Soon after Göbel died, Edison bought Göbel's "meritless" patent off Göbel's impoverished widow at a cost much lower than its worth.

Screwing over just one inventor might be all right for Galileo, but Edison was a dreamer. A year before Edison "invented" his lightbulb, Joseph Wilson Swan developed and patented a better bulb. When it became clear Edison's "this guy Swan's a lying asshole" defense wouldn't hold up in court, he made Swan a partner, forming the Edison & Swan United Electric Light Company (known as Ediswan), effectively buying Swan.

Thomas Edison: Father of the goddamned lightbulb.

Edison then used his incredible wealth to buy out Swan completely, leaving all records of the lightbulb under the care of the Edison Electric Light Company. Sure, Swan got rich in the end, but Edison purchased the right to claim he invented the lightbulb. Of course, there's a whole laundry list of inventors Edison stepped on, bullied, exploited, or convinced to name their price. But what do textbooks say about him?

Winston Rowntree

THE FIVE MOST FREQUENTLY QUOTED BULLSHIT STATISTICS

EVERY once in a while, we hear a statistic so startling we can't believe it's true. Our first impulse is to repeat it, because knowing interesting things tends to make people like us better. That's why facts tend to survive based on how interesting they are, rather than whether they're true.

The five most quoted "too awesome to be true" stats that are as fake as they sound:

5. YOU ONLY USE 10 PERCENT OF YOUR BRAIN

You've heard it since you were a child: We only use 10 percent of our brain. Just think what we'd be capable of if we could tap into the rest! It's appealing because it means that if we worked hard enough, we'd be able to set fires with the power of our minds.

Why is it a load of crap?

The parts of the brain are specialized, so trying to use all of it at once isn't going to make you smarter, just more confused. That's like trying to become a better writer by using every key on your keyboard all at once.

A series of neurologists over the past few hundred years figured out that a human can survive when parts of the brain are removed, which over time was misinterpreted to mean that the brain uses little of its potential, and the 10 percent statistic was born.

Who was fooled?

Not only do people still believe it, in 2006 *Psychology Today* even ran an article on how to access the lazy 90 percent of your gray matter.

One of the tips was to replenish the brain with nutrients, but we're assuming we get plenty with all the spiders we're eating every night. Oh, you didn't know?

4. YOU ACCIDENTALLY SWALLOW APPROXIMATELY EIGHT SPIDERS A YEAR

This commonly believed statistic has been fed to us by countless Internet chain emails: When you sleep, you open your mouth to breathe and supposedly this is the ideal window of opportunity for all the spiders who hang out near your bed, hoping to be eaten alive.

Winston Rowntree

Why is it a load of crap?

Back in 1993, *PC Professional* columnist Lisa Holst decided to prove that you could make up anything on the Internet and people would believe it.

She did this by putting together some utterly ridiculous "facts," the spider myth (taken from a collection of insect folklore that dates back to the 1950s) among them, and unleashing them on the world in the form of an email.

As Holst's email was forwarded from inbox to inbox, it began to evolve. The spider thing stayed, but somewhere along the line someone just "happened" to forget to include the fact that these facts were completely fake.

Who was fooled?

In 2006, the UK's *Daily Mirror* warned that "the average person will swallow anything from eight to 20 spiders before they die."

The *Mirror* then upped the ante by adding, "A spider is

also likely to drink from your eye at least *three* times in your life. Some experts have suggested they are attracted by the vibrations of snoring and the smell of undigested food—a good reason to floss your teeth before bedtime."

Really, is that what it takes to get the UK to worry about dental hygiene?

3. MEN THINK ABOUT SEX EVERY SIX SECONDS

As we all know, men do nothing but think about sex with their girlfriend or ex-girlfriend or friend who happens to be a girl/friend's sister. It follows, then, that on average men think about sex every six seconds, right?

Why is it a load of crap?

Hey, fellas, when you were reading the spider-eating segment, did you think about sex? Were you imagining a massive spider orgy? If so, you're alone (obviously). According to the Kinsey Institute, close to half of the men they surveyed said they don't even think about sex every day, let alone every six seconds. Even if men did think about sex that frequently, how would they be able to break it down to such a precise rate of perversion? Hook electrodes up to some dude's head and count how many times the sex lobe lights up in a week?

Who was fooled?

About half of us believe this fact, according to a 2007 poll conducted by mencanstoprape.org. It seems like common sense would have squashed this one even before it got started. Let's say you watched a four-hour marathon of *Matlock*, a show during which it is physically impossible to think about sex. To make up that average later, you'd have to think about sex every, what, two seconds? So for the rest of the day your brain would just turn into a spinning kaleidoscope of titty.

2. AFTER EATING YOU MUST WAIT THIRTY MINUTES BEFORE SWIMMING

For some families, the harsher "hour" rule was used. If you broke the rule, the fear was that you would get cramps, drown, and die. This statistic is apparently based on the assumption that water-to-skin contact will cause the food in your belly to explode.

Why is it a load of crap?
Because you're not a gremlin. As you may have already guessed, water does not bear properties that form a food-related cramp of death. Getting into the water after eating will have no more effect on your body than going for a walk.

This one's just an old wives' tale that slowly became popular over time. Supposedly, your stomach is using oxygen to digest food that your muscles need to swim. In actuality, the amount of oxygen your body needs to swim is more than satisfied, whether or not you've eaten.

Who was fooled?
Plenty of books and websites offer swimming tips that still buy into the thirty-minute rule. Go to any pool party with children, and we guarantee you'll hear someone's mother squawking about it.

1. CHRISTMAS CAUSES SUICIDE

It might be true that Christmas has become commercialized, but people generally seem to enjoy it. Aside from the stress, family you hate, travel, and the junk lying around the house, of course. And the music.

Winston Rowntree

When we hear that suicide rates jump during the holidays, it's easy to believe. Especially if you've ever spent a Christmas drunk and alone, eyes tearing as you sat in your apartment watching your favorite Christmas movie from childhood (*Die Hard*).

Why is it a load of crap?

According to Canada's Centre for Suicide Prevention, the suicide rate actually goes down significantly around the holidays.

While it's depressing as hell to be alone on Christmas, the truth is that most of us aren't. It's hard to commit suicide when there are people around constantly trying to get you to wear ugly sweaters. Depressed or not, most people aren't big enough dicks to let the kiddies find them hanging over the Christmas tree with a note pinned to their chest.

Who was fooled?

Just about every newspaper in the country tends to climb on board. In 1999, a press release was issued to major newspapers

114

warning against reporting the myth. During the holidays that same year, the Annenberg Public Policy Center found that two-thirds of newspaper articles mentioning the word *suicide* cited the mythical stat.

In the general population, whether or not you believe this stat tends to depend on how much you hate Christmas. When we're miserable, we like to project it on other people and assume they're all miserable too. And if thinking that other people are suicidal makes you feel a little less suicidal yourself, then go for it.

Jordan Monsell

THE FOUR MOST INSANE ATTEMPTS TO TURN NATURE INTO A WEAPON

NATURE inspires mankind's greatest ideas. The vivid colors of the setting sun might be reflected in an abstract masterpiece. The simple, rugged lines of a mountain range could serve as inspiration for an architectural wonder. The gentle caress of ocean waves lapping on the beach may be heard undulating in the symphonies of Mozart.

Or we could just shove nature into a gun and kill people with it. We do that a lot too.

4. BALL LIGHTNING CANNON

What is it?

Ball lightning is a phenomenon that usually occurs during thunderstorms and is often mistaken for fire or, in the South, a UFO. It's quite similar to ordinary lightning, but it's much rarer, lasts longer, and comes in a playful ball shape, presumably just to mess with your head. Science really doesn't know a ton about it, beyond the fact that it's astoundingly dangerous and notoriously unpredictable. So obviously scientists started trying to weaponize it the moment it was discovered. Nobody's gone public with how successful they have actually been, but Dr. Paul Koloc has been working on it for at least thirty years. Koloc's not one of those PhDs with pretentious fake goals like "advancing understanding" or "doing good"—no, his goal is now and has always been to create a functioning plasma cannon. He calls it the Phased Hyper-Acceleration for Shock, EMP, and Radiation, or PHASER, because he's a triple-threat guy: deadly, brilliant, and a giant nerd.

Christopher Hastings

117

A ball lightning–based weapon would theoretically destroy man and machine alike. It would be useful for shutting down electronics, shooting down missiles, stopping car engines, or just barbequing square-jawed do-gooders while the operator laughs maniacally and screams electricity-based puns from atop a giant robot spider.

Does it work?

Not yet! The problem isn't in creating the plasma itself—Dr. Koloc has been able to generate rings of various sizes for a while now—no, the problem is sustaining that plasma ring for a long enough period to kill someone dead. In part, this difficulty is because we don't know what ball lightning is exactly or how it works. And having even the vaguest understanding of something is a very helpful step when you're trying to put it in a gun and shoot planes out of the sky with it. So at this stage in the game, the military having a lightning cannon would be akin to a kindergartener owning a revolver that fires calculus.

3. DEEP DIGGER

What is it?

Chances are you've heard the term *bunker buster* before—the name of a bomb capable of destroying hardened underground structures, as well as a girl with a big ol' booty who knows how to use it (we made that one up, but we still stand behind it as a brilliant and accurate nickname). A typical bunker buster bomb has a timer that's activated once the bomb is released. The explosive is set to detonate only after the bomb has enough time to crash through a certain number of floors within a structure. The Deep Digger is the next logical step: Rather than simply crashing through your ceiling and exploding, the Digger actually propels itself through the earth or concrete—tunneling into bases—before it goes off.

And that's pretty terrifying, but where does nature come into all this? Well, the massive pulse created by the Deep Digger actually triggers a localized mini-earthquake upon detonation—collapsing tunnels, crushing subterranean bases, and probably pissing off any nearby Mole Men (but we'll cross that bridge when it rises from the earth to wreak vengeance on our children).

Does it work?

Oh yes, and their mass-production could mean the end of underground bunkers or underground anything that's not a Deep Digger, for that matter, in modern warfare. The newest version of the Deep Digger can reach depths of 150 feet, where, after separating into a group of twenty drilling warheads, they detonate and collapse all structures up to 300 feet below the surface for a 200-yard radius.

"But wait, couldn't bunkers be built below 300 feet?" you ask, because you're kind of a killjoy.

Yes, but there's something you're not thinking about: Every bunker needs an entrance leading to the surface. The damage isn't done by exploding the bunker; it's done by sealing the earth around the people inside of it. So, if you want to be technical about it, the Deep Digger is a nonlethal weapon like mace or tear gas; that is, if mace buried you and your friends alive until you suffocated or cannibalized each other.

2. THE SUN GUN

What is it?

During World War II the Germans were developing a series of whimsically named *Wunderwaffen*, or "wonder weapons," which, despite sounding like a warfare strategy developed by the Care Bears, were actually terrifying. These *Wunderwaffen* were designed to be both practical and theatrical—intimidating foes while also killing the shit out of them. If you gathered up every Bond villain superweapon and whipped them into a mixture of dubious science and murder, added a dash of the occult, and baked it in an oven preheated to clown-shit-crazy degrees, you'd get the sun gun. Originally designed in 1929, the sun gun was pretty simple: A space station in orbit held a hundred-meter-wide mirror, which it used to focus concentrated sunlight on any point on the planet. It was like a gargantuan Nazi child roasting human ants with his space magnifying glass, if that helps you picture it.

Did it work?

If you're reading this right now, chances are your grandparents weren't melted alive by space Nazis—but that isn't because the mirror didn't work; the Nazis just never finished building it. There weren't enough resources (or spaceflight) at the time, but researchers were able to determine the necessary size required of a mirror to burn up a city and even what materials they could use to construct it.

During Allied interrogation, those working on the sun gun stated that it was all merely a matter of time and manpower to get a fully functioning prototype. They weren't wrong of course. It just would have taken much more time and manpower than they could muster. Seeing as these were the same people who thought Hitler was an awesome boss and that the "nation" of Poland was more of a suggestion, really, nobody was too surprised when it turned out they were full of shit.

1. THE VORTEX CANNON

What is it?

Another *Wunderwaffen*, or Willy Wonka's weapons of whimsy, the vortex cannon worked on the idea that even small-scale turbulence could knock fighter planes out of the sky. The Nazis figured if they could create turbulent skies on demand, they could economize on the massive resources they spent building shells for antiaircraft artillery and start really getting serious about the giant sun laser. A Nazi scientist named Dr. Zimmermeyer developed the first version of the vortex cannon, which was astoundingly simple technology considering we're talking about a tornado gun: A giant mortar barrel was sunk into the ground and loaded with shells containing coal dust, hydrogen, and oxygen. When the shells detonated, they would create a mini-vortex strong enough to bring down any planes within a hundred meters and cause everybody witnessing it to quit the war because "dark wizardry" isn't covered under the Geneva Conventions.

Did it work?

Holy shit . . . yes?! At one point in history, the Nazi forces had a functioning tornado gun they used to whirl planes out of the sky? Presumably Indiana Jones got to them before it could be deployed, as that is the only conceivable reason why we won the war against the Axis of Ridiculous Superweapons.

Well, actually it was because the gun didn't work nearly as reliably as conventional antiaircraft weaponry. Considering the whole appeal of the vortex cannon was that it was supposed to consume fewer resources than a normal gun to take down a plane, the Axis decided to stick with the stupid, boring old explosive shells.

So really, it all boils down to this: The only reason you're not living in a fantastical comic book world of wacky doomsday devices is because the people in accounting ran the numbers, and supervillainy, while totally feasible, was just too damned expensive.

THE FOUR GREATEST THINGS EVER ACCOMPLISHED WHILE HIGH

REMEMBER DARE? Those brave police officers came into your school and told you nothing good ever came from drugs? They were lying too.

4. FRANCIS CRICK DISCOVERS DNA THANKS TO LSD

Francis Crick is the closest the field of genetics gets to a rock star, which it turns out is pretty damn close. In 1953, he burst through the front door of his Cambridge home and told his wife, Odile, to draw two spirals twisting in opposite directions from one another. She drew what he described, having no clue that her sketch would become the most reproduced drawing in the history of science: a first draft of the double helix structure of DNA that scientists today still describe as "balls on."

The drug: LSD

When not discovering the key to life, and winning the Nobel Prize for it, Crick spent the 1950s and '60s throwing all-night parties famous for featuring that era's favorite party favors: LSD and bare-naked breasts. Crick never made it a secret that he experimented with the drug, and in 2006 the London *Mail on Sunday* reported that Crick had told many colleagues that he was experimenting with LSD when he figured out the double helix structure.

Why it makes sense

The double helix is essentially the *Sgt. Pepper's* of scientific models, a ladder that's been melted and twirled by a pasta fork, or the two snakes from the caduceus if one of them was boning the other with a hundred dicks (depending on whether the artist ate the good or bad acid). Now, obviously scientists don't arrive at models by doodling on their Trapper Keepers and picking out the shape that looks the coolest. Crick was a fan of Aldous Huxley's *The Doors of Perception*, a study of the human mind undertaken, like all good studies, while driving around LA on mescaline.

Huxley wrote that the sober mind has a series of filters on it that basically prevent abstract thought. Evolution put them there to keep you from plowing your car into a tree while gazing at the mind-blowing beauty of its foliage. But Huxley and

Crick thought drugs like mescaline and LSD could temporarily remove those filters. So rather than melting his mind into a lava lamp of trippy shapes, Crick probably used LSD to get unfiltered access to a part of his brain most normal people rarely use.

Before you go trying it...

While Crick never officially wore a tinfoil hat, he was known to argue that life was seeded on earth by a race of prehistoric aliens, a theory that has yet to gain widespread acceptance among the scientific community or really anyone who isn't a character on *The X-Files* or a member of the Church of Scientology.

3. FREUD AND COCAINE INVENT PSYCHOANALYSIS

Freudian psychoanalysis is one of the most influential and controversial theories of the twentieth century. While you can argue its merits all day, you can't deny that it created an entire branch of medicine and, more important, gave us the two best seasons of *The Sopranos*.

The drug: cocaine

The first ten years of Sigmund Freud's career were like a roving cocaine pep rally. He wrote cocaine prescriptions for his friends with headaches, nasal ailments, or just to "give [their] cheeks a red color." He wrote cocaine-fueled love letters to his wife in which he referred to himself as a "wild man with cocaine in his blood." Oh, and he also published a paper called *On Coca*, wherein the basic thesis was: Cocaine is freaking awesome. You should really think about trying some.

After one of his friends overdosed on the drug, Freud quietly folded up his cocaine pom-poms and sweater-skirt combo, and went on to found the theory that bears his name. But according to Freud biographer Louis Berger, it may also have played a part in the less-embarrassing second act of his career.

Why it makes sense

Apparently, before cocaine Freud was an emotionally sterile, socially awkward lab rat. Flash forward to a series of all-night cocaine benders in which Freud and his friend Fleischel stayed up all night discussing their "profoundest despair."

Scarfreud 2: Freudface

Anthony Clark

This probably sounds familiar to anyone who's been around people on the drug or has at least seen the movie *Boogie Nights.* Cocaine gives you a preternatural ability to talk about yourself, and according to Berger (who is a professor emeritus of psychoanalytic studies at the California Institute of Technology), it was responsible for Freud's enthusiasm for discussing how you feel about your mother.

Before you go trying it...

Fleischel, the friend who sent Freud on the path toward psychoanalysis, was also the friend the drug ended up killing.

2. A COKE ADDICT MAKES A COKE-FLAVORED COLA AND CALLS IT COKE

Coca-Cola is the biggest brand in the history of the world. Sure, it's mostly just soda water and sugar, but they sell about 400 billion cans of the stuff a year, an average of more than sixty cans to every single human being on the planet.

The drug: Coke has it right there in the name

When Coca-Cola was invented in the summer of 1885, sodas were advertised for their health benefits. Dr. Pepper got its name from the Texas physician who marketed it as a cure for impotence. Coca-Cola was able to stand out in the crowded market because its purported side effects weren't total and utter bullshit.

John Pemberton, the Atlanta pharmacist who invented Coca-Cola, named it after the coca leaf, one of the ingredients he claimed cured everything from depression and nervousness to morphine addiction. If that sales pitch sounds familiar, congratulations, you could beat a chimpanzee in a game of memory. Coca is the leaf that produces cocaine, and like Freud, John Pemberton was a big fan.

Why it makes sense

Pemberton said he was convinced from "actual experiments that coca is the very best substitute for opium addicts." Of course, he was speaking from personal experience, since he himself was a junky who used cocaine to kick the habit.

In his book *For God, Country, and Coca-Cola*, Mark Pendergrast claims there were about 8.45 milligrams of cocaine in each serving, which is about one-quarter of what people put up their nose to get high these days. But fans of the drink were

YOU **MIGHT** BE A **ZOMBIE** AND OTHER **BAD** NEWS

known to chug up to five at a sitting, or to drink the syrup instead of mixing it with water, both practices that would bring the high to right around street level.

So how instrumental was the drug in making Coke the largest brand on earth? By the time they removed its magic ingredient, in the early twentieth century, addicts were ordering the wildly popular beverage by asking for "a dope."

Before you go trying it...

Turns out Pemberton was wrong about cocaine's ability to cure morphine addiction. According to Pendergrast, the year he died he was so "worried about where money would come from for his morphine" that "John Pemberton sold two-thirds of his Coca-Cola rights . . . for the grand sum of one dollar." Of course, that's one dollar in 1888 money. Today, that'd be worth not even *one goddamned billionth* of what you should leave your family after inventing the most successful product in the history of capitalism!

1. DOCK ELLIS TRIPS HIS WAY TO A NO-HITTER

In the hundreds of thousands of games in Major League Baseball history, there have been only 267 in which the starting pitcher completes a game without giving up a hit. Pedro Martínez, like most pitchers, has gone his entire career without throwing one. In fact, the New York Mets have been sending a pitcher out to the mound 162 times every season for forty-six years, and not a single one has pitched one. Pittsburgh Pirates pitcher Dock Ellis did it on June 20, 1970, though he barely remembers being there.

The drug: acid

The day of his no-hitter, Dock Ellis woke up around noon on what he thought was Friday and ate three tabs of acid. When his girlfriend arrived carrying Saturday's newspaper, Ellis realized that either his girlfriend was a time traveler or he'd slept through Friday. The sports page had more bad news—he was scheduled to pitch in San Diego in six hours. Not only had he woken up on the wrong day, but the city that was just starting to swim around him was Los Angeles.

Unfazed, Ellis hopped a flight to San Diego and faced down a lineup that had woken up knowing what day it was and also had the upper hand in the "not on acid" category.

Not a single one got a hit.

Ellis remembers very little about the game, other than that sometimes the ball looked huge and other times tiny, and that at one point he dove out of the way of a line drive, only to look up and see that the ball hadn't even reached the mound.

Why it makes sense

Writing in the *New Yorker*, Oliver Sacks describes a state of mind known among athletes as "the zone" in which, "A baseball . . . approaching at close to a hundred miles per hour . . . may seem to be almost immobile in the air, its very seams strikingly visible . . . in a suddenly enlarged and spacious timescape." The zone is typically brought on by confidence, adrenaline, and being freaking awesome at baseball. Ellis was all of those things, and LSD's effects include increased heart rate and the perception that time has slowed. So it's conceivable that Ellis tripped his way into the zone.

There's also the mental component. A large part of throwing a no-hitter is getting over the fact that you're doing it. As the game goes on and the lonely bastard in the middle of

"Time to pitch at baseball! Watch it throw, today! Sports forever!"

the diamond gets closer to immortality, the tension builds in the park and in the pitcher. Trying to throw a no-hitter is so mentally taxing that it's considered the height of dickery for a teammate to acknowledge it until the final out is recorded.

But baseball history was the last thing on Ellis's mind that day. He was too busy trying to keep his shit together while a bunch of giant lizards had an orgy in the on-deck circle.

Before you go trying it...
Ellis never reached his potential because of drug addiction. Instead of being a household name, he's just that guy who threw a no-hitter on acid.

Anthony Clark

FOUR MYTHOLOGICAL BEASTS
THAT ACTUALLY EXIST

CRYPTOZOOLOGY, according to cryptozoologists, is the study of heretofore undiscovered species. According to everybody else, it's what lunatics who prefer lying in the international language of science call the animals they make up. Bigfoot is the spawn of cryptozoologists, for instance. It's pretty much a bullshit factory, but every so often real researchers discover that the terrified villagers were warning them about that monster because it's *right behind them.* These are the terrifying myths that turned out to be terrifying realities.

4. THE KRAKEN: MONSTER FROM THE DEEP

The myth

The word *kraken* is simply German for "octopus." Kind of a letdown, right? An octopus isn't very scary; it's more like the physical manifestation of pubescent awkwardness—all flailing limbs and messy secretions—but as with many monsters, it's really just a matter of scale. Nothing is cute when it's big enough to eat your house, and the kraken is no exception.

For years sailors have been returning to harbor with stories of a giant tentacled beast. Some said that it was more than a mile in diameter. Others claimed that it was the first animal made in all of creation and would only perish when the world ended. We tended to relegate tales of the kraken to the same bin of bullshit where we throw mermaids and the Loch Ness monster—or at least we did until a few years ago, when a bunch of New Zealand fisherman hauled one into their boat.

The reality

It's called the colossal squid. Now, we tend to get a bit unnerved by anything that scientists decide to label *colossal*, because they're a moderate bunch. In the realm of science, something only gets dubbed as colossal because the textbooks frown on classifying animals as being of the genus *F**kmassive holyshitbricks*.

And the colossal squid is not just a name: It's a thirty-foot-long flailing engine of nightmares. Scientists excitedly tell us of its oddities, such as tentacles lined with "sharp, swiveling, three-pointed hooks," and how the 1,091-pound specimen on display in New Zealand is thought to be "much smaller than average."

It's not like it's a peaceful behemoth that we're giving a hard time due to its appearance. Comparing the smaller-than-average specimen the fisherman hauled in to the largest squid thought possible prior to 1997, experts from Auckland University of Technology noted, "The Colossal Squid, with the hooks and the beak that it has, not only is colossal in size but is going to be a phenomenal predator," before helpfully clarifying that this made it "something you are not going to want to meet in the water."

So no, ancient mariners weren't just being quaint when they marked the deep sea as "here there be monsters" on their maps; it was just shorter than writing "here there be thirty-foot-tall multilimbed, razor-hooked fury beasts that look like a giant, wet bag of violence, and you should probably just stay home until somebody invents faster boats."

3. IRKUIEM: THE GOD-BEAR

The myth

There could be all manner of bizarre creatures living in Siberia, the frigid wilderness that covers 10 percent of the earth's land. Human beings didn't really bother to set up proper civilizations out there. To this day, explorers come back from the Siberian hinterlands with tall tales about giant reptiles, living mammoths, and enough yetis to populate some kind of yeti academy. Mixed in with all that bullshit was the god-bear.

The reality

In 1936, a Swedish zoologist named Sten Bergman ventured into Siberia and started to hear stories about so-called monster bears. After Bergman mussed the hair of a few tribal elders while saying, "Sure, buddy. Did he come out from under your bed?" the natives showed him pelts, skulls, and paw prints larger than those of any known bear in the region. That's when science collectively stopped rolling its eyes and making wanking motions, and began taking the god-bear seriously.

It just so happens that the villagers' description matched that of an immense prehistoric horror called the short-faced bear (*Arctodus simus*), one of the largest predatory mammals to ever exist. A Soviet zoologist named Dr. Nikolai Vereshchagin postulated that *Arctodus*, thought extinct for twelve thousand years, was actually alive and well in Siberia.

Other scientists have theorized that the god-bear is actually a colony of enormous black polar bears that found their way too far south and found the villagers delicious enough to stick around. One way or another, Siberia sounds entirely too much like a frozen version of the island from *Lost*.

Even if reports of a real, live god-bear are false, anthropologists agree that they probably didn't die off *that* long ago. But why would there still be stories about the creatures if they no longer exist? In most cases, we'd go with "people are full of shit," but when you're talking about a giant man-eating bear, we're willing to make allowances for post-traumatic stress disorder so severe it's become hereditary.

2. BUAJA DARAT: THE LAND CROCODILE

The myth

The East had always been a strange and mysterious place in the eyes of the West, and many tall tales emerged to keep whitey baffled and entertained while he butchered the locals. One of these legends was the Indonesian land crocodile, or *buaja darat*: A fearsome lizard-monster that lived on the nearby islands. The *buaja darat* could eat a man whole if necessary, but even a single bite from the creature was fatal. That's why nobody survived to verify accounts firsthand.

But then the tales started to come true: In 1912, a group of fisherman docked on a small Indonesian island called Komodo and came back half-eaten and raving about monsters. After a 1926 expedition by W. Douglas Burden yielded twelve preserved specimens science finally woke up and realized *there are actually dragons.* They are a thing that exists. They're just over in Southeast Asia. And they hate you.

The reality

The Komodo dragon is not only the largest lizard in the world; it's also one of the few animals that will just up and eat you. We're not talking about incidents born out of self-defense; we're talking about an animal that is a hard-core fan of murder and not such a hard-core fan of your uneaten face.

That stuff about a single bite killing you? The dragon's saliva has venom that will prevent your blood from clotting. Even if you escape, it can just follow you at a leisurely pace, eyeing you with that dickish, lizardy expression while you panic and bleed out into delicious human jerky.

The only reason Komodo dragons haven't eaten everyone you care about yet is because there are so few of them, and they all exist on the one island. But then again, we remember a movie about a bunch of giant carnivorous lizards contained on a small island, and that didn't exactly end in hugs and milk shakes.

1. POUAKAI: MAN-EATING EAGLE

The myth

The Maori people of New Zealand are basically a death-metal video in human packaging and have the most hard-core monster legends around. Like Pouakai the bird god. Or, as we prefer: the giant man-eating eagle (of death). The Maoris have many stories about this sky demon. They say it would perch out of sight of villages and swoop down to pick people off one by one until entire tribes were killed off. It was said that the last thing the victims heard was the deafening beating of its immense wings, possibly followed by whatever sound a skull collapsing makes, and then the mournful drizzle of fear urine. Surely such a monstrosity never existed under the same sun as human beings, for our God is a kind god and not prone to creating stealth bombers carved from flesh that think men are delicious, right?

Anthony Clark

The reality

Roughly one hundred thousand years ago, Australia was populated by megafauna, which basically means that all the cute and cuddly animals of today were huge and terrifying. New Zealand, probably overcompensating for millennia of being overshadowed by Australia, had something called Haast's eagle: the largest bird of prey to ever exist.

When human beings finally breezed in from the wider world to find most of New Zealand's megafauna at the sizes we know of today, they were probably pretty stoked to find an island without lions and god-bears and whatever other massive predators thought it was hilarious that these soft pink monkeys tried to run away from them. Boy, were they in for a tragic, terrifying surprise!

Researchers believe Haast's eagle was almost certainly the origin of the Pouakai stories.

So that would mean all the horrifying shit that flashed through your imagination a few paragraphs ago—the flapping wings, the fear urine, the entire tribes picked off one by one like slasher-flick victims—that all probably happened.

Although, after a few generations of devouring humans for fun and profit, mankind did finally have the last laugh at Haast's eagle: We drove it to extinction simply by eating everything else around it and then not providing enough nutrition with our doughy little bodies to sustain the notoriously ravenous diet of the bird gods.

So, yeah . . . *Suck it*, enormous sky raptor of legend! We beat your ass by not having enough calories! Go humanity!

FIVE WAYS YOUR BRAIN IS MESSING WITH YOUR HEAD

SURE, our minds are being screwed with by advertisers, politicians, magicians, etc. But as it turns out, the ways in which your head is being truly and royally messed with the most are coming from inside your skull.

5. CHANGE BLINDNESS

Change blindness is the inability to notice changes that happen right in front of you as long as you don't watch the actual change take place.

Um, what?

Focus on anyone around you. If their pants spontaneously changed color, you'd notice and probably soil your own. But if you looked away and focused on something else, then came back and found their jeans had turned to khakis, odds are you almost certainly would not notice, even if your attention was elsewhere for only a few seconds.

If your brain processed everything in your visual spectrum you would go insane, so instead it picks and chooses what to focus on. If an image changes while your brain isn't paying attention, your brain tells you the change was there all along.

It's like your brain is sitting in class, staring out the window at a cloud that sort of looks like a penis. When you call on your brain, it does the same thing you do when a teacher calls on you in those circumstances: starts bullshitting.

Where it gets really weird ...

Working with psychologist Susan Greenfield, the BBC decided to take this idea to a ridiculous extreme. They filmed an experiment in which one man worked the counter at a university copy center while another hid below the counter. When a student walked up and requested a form, the first man would duck down behind the counter to get it, and the previously hidden man would pop up and say, "Ah, here it is." Despite this previously hidden second person looking completely different, most of the students did not freaking notice that they were now talking to a totally different person.

This is probably what made the producers of *Bewitched* think they could just switch Darrins on us.

4. SACCADIC MASKING

Saccadic masking is the forty or so minutes per day that you're effectively blind.

Um, what?

Look at the wall to your left. When you flicked your eyes over there, for just a moment you were blind. And you didn't even know it.

Ever watch a movie that gave you motion sickness due to the camera whipping around too fast with that "shaky handheld camera" gimmick? Your brain doesn't like those rapid changes in vision, which is why some folks ended up puking while watching *Cloverfield*.

Your eye movements are even faster and shakier than that. If you were to look closely at someone else's eye, you'd notice that it's never steady for more than a third of a second. Even when you think you're rolling your eyes, they're actually moving in a series of rapid jerky movements known as saccades. To prevent your world from looking like you're seeing it through a jerky camcorder all day, your brain shuts down your optic nerve during these tiny movements. That's why we told you to look at your friend's eyeball instead of looking at your own in a mirror. While it might have created less sexual tension, everyone's own eyeball will look perfectly stationary to them because they're blind during each and every jerky saccade. That's saccadic masking.

Where it really gets weird . . .

The spooky part is the way your brain prevents you from noticing the blackness that occurs several times a second, every time you use your eyes. Estimates vary, but it's likely that you're spending around forty minutes a day with your eyes wide open, and totally blind.

Here's where saccadic masking and change blindness team up to screw with your mind. A scientist named George McConkie was able to track people's eye movements down to each individual saccadic movement. This enabled him to introduce changes in words and text without the subject noticing *while they were looking directly at it.* If a change occurs during that fraction of a second when the brain is dodging calls like the optic nerve was an ex-girlfriend, you won't notice it. Even when it happens right in front of your damned eyes.

Winston Rowntree

3. PROPRIOCEPTION

Proprioception is your brain's map of your body, and it steers you wrong on a regular basis.

Um, what?

Proprioception is your brain's ability to sense where your limbs are. This is how you can put a sandwich in your mouth while your eyes are focused on the TV: Your brain knows where your hand is in relation to your face.

If you've ever failed a field sobriety test, you know this kind of self-knowledge is fallible. Your proprioception is like your brain's underwear: pretty much the first thing to disappear when you're any kind of drunk. Basically, the cops doing the roadside test are trying to see if your brain knows where your fingers are in relation to your nose.

Even though your brain carries around a detailed awareness of exactly where your body parts are at all times, when that awareness gets drunk enough to start lying to you, you'll ignore everything you've ever known and say, "Oh, well. Guess I've been wrong about the length of my nose all these years."

Where it really gets weird . . .

The best example we've found so far is "the Pinocchio illusion." Scientists have found that they can have the subject touch the tip of their nose with their finger while having their biceps electrically stimulated at the same time. Your brain "feels" your arm muscle extending, but also feels that you're maintaining contact with the tip of your nose and leaps to the immediate conclusion that your nose has suddenly grown to be about three feet long.

Incidentally, we know exactly which illusion you're about to try to induce, figuring all it'll take is a girl, a dark room, and the right equipment. Don't do it. It leads to eventual disappointment.

2. CRYPTOMNESIA

Sometimes called *subconscious plagiarism*, it's what happens when your brain rips off someone else's ideas and doesn't tell you.

Um, what?

Your brain isn't great at remembering where your ideas come from. Cryptomnesia happens when you find a really good idea and don't bother to remember that it's not yours.

Although occurrences are pretty rare, there are still some famous cases: Nietzsche accidentally didn't write quite a bit of *Thus Spoke Zarathustra*, George Harrison was forced to shell out almost $600,000 for a song he "borrowed," and an early incident with cryptomnesia permanently ruined the celebrity-author career of Helen Keller, who wrote up a fairy tale that it turned out had been told to her years before—much to her surprise.

This occurs when your brain retains enough memory to recall an event but not the origin of the event, leading to the convenient and mistaken impression that you're the originator.

You may be wondering at this point how we know cryptomnesia exists at all. After all, how do we know those cases of "accidental" plagiarism weren't all intentional?

The answer: We don't. If you haven't experienced it for yourself, you have no way of knowing whether it's not just a big fat scam. If you have experienced it, good luck trying to convince that first group.

Where it really gets weird . . .

But there is plenty of evidence that we're really bad at remembering where our ideas come from. In 2002, the journal *Psychological Science* published an experiment in which scientists implanted a completely fabricated childhood memory in the minds of subjects. The researchers showed the subjects a doctored photograph that depicted them in the basket of a hot-air balloon. Even though the subjects had never been in a hot-air balloon, many of them constructed detailed memories to match the fake photograph.

So no matter how confident you are in the originality of an idea, it's worth Googling around to make sure you didn't inadvertently steal it. Also, no matter how unlikely it might seem, scientists will take the time to Photoshop you into a hot-air balloon, just to screw with your head.

1. SUBCONSCIOUS BEHAVIOR, A.K.A. BEST GUESSING

When you're running down a flight of stairs at top speed, your brain doesn't have time to think about each and every step you take. Your feet are on autopilot, reaching out for the next step faster than your conscious mind can tell them what to do. Well, it turns out that your brain is on autopilot more often than you think. Even when you're making important choices throughout the course of your day, a part of your brain knows what you're going to do well before it lets your conscious mind in on the decision. The technical term for this: *precognition.*

Um, what?

Your brain is constantly making guesses and predictions about what's happening or about to happen around you, and once it has a good idea of what it thinks is about to go down, it acts on that prediction before you've made a conscious choice to act. In some cases, it will move parts of your body. Other times it will screw with your perception.

If it didn't do this, we'd be the clumsiest creatures on the planet. Our brains have to make thousands of snap decisions throughout the day. Imagine if you needed to consciously decide to put one foot in front of the other while flying down those steps. Luckily, there's a part of your brain that's constantly making decisions you only find out about after they occur. The creepy part is that you don't get to decide when it's time to use autopilot.

Take the starburst illusion to the right. It takes advantage of the fact that your brain has *lots* of experience with converging lines. When we "see" the background starburst pattern in real life, we're generally traveling toward a point of convergence, on a road or down a tunnel for instance. But no matter how much you try to convince your autopilot to shut the hell up, your brain adjusts your perception by enlarging and distorting the center, as though you were moving toward it. That's why those perfectly vertical lines look like they're bending outward in the middle.

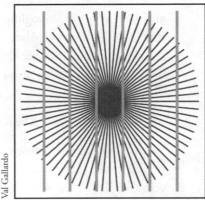

Val Gallardo

Where it really gets weird...

In 2008, the *Wall Street Journal* reported on a series of experiments being conducted with brain scanners in Germany, Norway, and the United States. The scientists found that if they hook you up to a scanner and ask you to make a decision, part of your brain lights up to take action up to ten seconds before you consciously make the decision. So when you're working out in your head whether or not to go to work tomorrow, a part of your brain has already decided to call in sick, several seconds before the voice in your head arrives at that same conclusion.

Think about what that means for free will, and prepare to have your mind blown (it should hit you in about ten seconds).

FIVE FIGHT MOVES THAT ONLY WORK IN MOVIES

MOVIEGOERS understand that *most* of what they're seeing in action flicks is bullshit: Buses won't jump a sixty-yard gap in the highway, a fire hose is not a bungee cord, and Steven Seagal is a bigger threat to a Sizzler buffet than a gang of criminals. Objectively, our brains *know* that, and yet most real-world bar fights feature at least one guy trying out a move he saw in a martial arts film—and being subsequently shocked to learn he would have been better off casting an ass-kicking spell he'd found in the pages of a Harry Potter novel.

5. BEER BOTTLE OVER THE HEAD

For years, a beer bottle shattered over the head has been the visual shorthand for "this person got knocked unconscious." But when real people really smack a real beer bottle over someone's head, one of two things happens: (1) It doesn't break and they are enraged, or (2) their head gets wet. If you're lucky, you might open up a cut. If you're unlucky, it will be on your hand. Otherwise the body attached to the head it broke against can go about the business of kicking your ass while still fully conscious and, if anything, somewhat refreshed.

You don't have to take our word for it: Thanks to YouTube and the contents of the beer bottles themselves, there are hundreds of easily accessible failed bottle-over-head experiments. And though each of the amateur scientists involved clearly has a soft skull, they all remain wildly undevastated by their bottle-breaking field work. No one's saying try this at home, just trust that the millions of years evolution spent building a helmet for your brain trumps an empty Bud Light every time.

The rest of *Road House* though? One hundred percent accurate. It's basically a documentary.

4. THE TWIST WITH YOUR HANDS/LEGS NECK BREAK

Even if you do it *really hard* and your victim is a *completely* incidental guard outside the enemy's base, coming up behind someone and cranking their head to the side doesn't break their neck. You probably suspected this the

Robert Bogl

first time your chiropractor did it to you and you didn't wake up rolling through heaven in a wheelchair. When the spine is given a choice between simply turning in the same direction as the neck or detaching from the head, it usually picks the first one.

But what if you leap up, wrap your legs around his head, and kind of twist? Surely something that awesome-looking has to be effective! Well, no. And what's worse, the mythical leg-scissors neck break actually squanders a golden opportunity to do some *real* damage. If you find yourself in a position to execute a leg-around-the-head move, modern jujitsu would recommend a tight triangle choke, thus matching the puny muscles of your opponent's neck against your comparatively immense leg muscles. If you instead take your pointers from Jean-Claude Van Damme movies and just twist your hips awkwardly, you'll be astonished at how much your opponent doesn't die. In fact, you'll be lucky if you manage to give him an Indian burn with your jeans before he takes advantage of the prime penis-biting position you've put him in. In short: No one will be dead and you'll both go home with a lot of explaining to do to your wives.

3. THE STANDING ARM-BREAK

If Steven Seagal blocks your punch, there's a really good chance you're going to be the bad type of double jointed in the very near future. Whether he's cracking arms over his shoulder or kicking knees in the wrong direction, all extremities turn to crispy breadsticks under Seagal's awesome powers. According to martial arts movies, a half pound of pressure shatters a kneecap, while according to real life Hollywood got all its information on bones well before the invention of milk.

It takes a lot more than yanking on an arm to break it. Two much more likely things happen first: Either the body attached to the arm goes in the direction you pull it, or the shoulder simply dislocates. Trying to snap the bone before one of these things happens is like trying to knock a wall down by jumping into the window.

There is actual documentation of a forced arm-breaking, but it took more than Steven Seagal gently leaning his considerable bulk against an elbow to make it happen. At UFC 48: Payback, jujitsu expert Frank Mir locked his entire 250-pound body onto Tim Sylvia's arm and cranked it as hard as he could, while six-foot-eight Sylvia stood up and pulled in the opposite direction. His forearm snapped. To re-create these kinds of conditions outside the ring, you'd need a gallon of moonshine, a tractor, and the world's dumbest volunteer.

2. KNOCKING A NOSE INTO A BRAIN

In 1991's *The Last Boy Scout*, Bruce Willis punched a henchman so hard he died. Another henchman exclaimed, "God, he punched his nose through his brains!" From that moment on, filmmakers no longer felt the need to explain why their characters die after getting hit in the nose. In reality, the henchman's buddy might as well have screamed, "God, Bruce Willis hired elves to eat their way into his skull! They've made it into a cookie factory!"

The human nose does not contain the brain's off button. It's made of soft cartilage. In the history of face punching, people have probably died, but it was not from a nose's soft tissue traveling through skull bone and lobotomizing its owner. That would be like trying to hammer a crayon through a brick wall. If you finally break through, it ain't gonna be the crayon that does the trick. That's why you could get punched all day and you'd still have a better chance of dying from a winning lottery ticket falling out of the sky and slicing your wrist open than from a face-to-brain nose missile.

1. ALMOST ANY KICK YOU'VE EVER SEEN IN A MOVIE

Attackers are charging at you from both sides! Before you decide to leap into the air and kick them each at the same time, you should know that's only going to make you go out looking like a cheerleader. A kick's power is generated by your hips, and your hips can't generate any power while they're spreading in midair, thirsting for a man's touch.

Most kicks in movies are designed around aesthetics rather than effectiveness. If Jean-Claude Van Damme was trying to break down the front door of your house, he wouldn't twirl into the air and kick the door. It's easier and more effective to kick the door in like a regular person, with one foot planted firmly on the ground (also, Van Damme would just come back as *Timecop* and hand himself the key). The one and only strategic advantage the door has is that it's connected to something that's connected to the ground. So are you, until you leap in the air like *Crouching Tiger, Hidden Dragon* and earn every bullet of the Darwinian reckoning about to be visited on you by the drug dealer who just heard you bounce off his front door.

The same goes for real combat. In Ultimate Fighting, all but two kicks have become extinct: the round kick (what it sounds like) and the front kick (what you should have done to the door a few sentences ago). If you are practicing a kick that involves a word like *spinning, crescent, flying,* or *cartwheel,* remember it'll only be useful in a real fight when you want to fall down extravagantly before getting choked.

CAUTION

THE SAND IS ABSOLUTELY
FULL OF TURDS

Anthony Clark

FIVE AWESOME PLACES TO HAVE SEX (AND THE HORRIFIC CONSEQUENCES)

EVERY month magazines like *Cosmo*, *Playboy*, and *Boob Fancy* write up titillating articles about places you just *have* to have sex at least once in your life. All of them seem to operate on the principle that having sex while, say, zooming down the Pacific Coast Highway on a motorcycle is well worth the risks involved.

You should at least know the dangers before you get drunk enough to try five of the most popular.

5. SEX ON THE BEACH

Sex on the beach *sounds* pretty hot. It's so popular that there's even a drink named after it. Then again, there's also a drink named the duck fart. In any event, it's still a common motif in romantic films and books. What could be more romantic than some briny coitus between two half-naked adults while the waves crash around your suntanned bodies?

Just about anything, it turns out. As anyone who's ever had sex on the beach probably already knows, if you're not extremely careful, you're going to discover what it feels like to exfoliate areas of your body you can't see without a mirror. And while places that recommend sex on the beach will point out the sand issue with a little wink and a nudge, they rarely mention one important detail about the sand you're cramming into your unmentionable areas: It's often loaded with fecal bacteria.

Sand acts as a naturally occurring filth filter, so when a beach is closed due to high bacteria levels in the water, the sand is what makes it safe to swim again, collecting big, fatty loads of turd with the ebb and flow of tides. Good news for the surfers, swimmers, and the mayor of Amity Island. It's even good for the bacteria, which live fuller, more robust lives in the sand than in the ocean. The news is less good for couples grinding sand around one another's sexual organs like a human pepper mill. Exposure to the bacteria can lead to fun things like typhoid fever, hepatitis A, and dysentery, all terrible diseases even when they're not focused in your nether regions.

4. IN A POOL

Of course you could always dodge nature's poo filter by having some good clean sex in a far more sanitary (looking) chlorinated swimming pool. What could be hotter than dipping your naked hide in clear azure water, while a pool noodle bobs obscenely along with your ungainly and hard-to-maintain humping?

It turns out pool sex has the unwholesome side effect of teaching you just how poorly water works as a lubricant while forcing chemically treated liquids deep into easily infected regions. According to research by the University of California, Santa Barbara, if turkey basted into the wrong places, even chlorinated pool water contains enough bacteria to lead to yeast and urinary tract infections.

The aforementioned issue with lubrication leads to something science types call *microtears* but that you're going to be more likely to call "tiny, painful rips in my junk." That's why having sex in a pool greatly increases the risk of STDs and, more disastrously, pruny zombie wang.

If you're looking to avoid chlorine with some manner of ocean scuba sex, dive researcher David F. Colvard, MD, would like you to know that having sex underwater can lead to your losing track of important things like buoyancy. You could end up floating to the surface too quickly, giving yourself an embolism. Now, we're not underwater sex doctors, like Dr. Colvard back there, but an embolism is probably a total willy wilter.

3. IN A CAR

The idea of getting nasty in a car, or *road head*, as Mom used to call it, is a staple of the not-so-exotic fantasy life of many people. Back in the 1950s, everyone was taking their girl up to make-out point to pump her full of babies on luxurious leather upholstery. As time went on, people apparently decided parked-car sex simply didn't endanger enough lives and moved on to having sex while driving. Hey, who doesn't like a little eroticism to break up the monotony of steering a fast-moving chunk of metal and flammable liquids?

How about the innocent bystander, whose last memory is being plowed into by a Subaru full of naked humping yuppie? When a Connecticut woman was charged with causing a car wreck that killed a man, she tried to use the fact that she was mid-blow-job in her defense. While it's unclear what reaction she was hoping for ("Oh, she had a dick in her mouth, well, happens to the best of us I suppose!"), the argument only helped convince the jury that her mother and father had failed as parents.

Even humping in the back of a taxi carries risks beyond making a cameo on HBO. Unless you're grotesquely double jointed, it's pretty hard to wear a seat belt while having sex, and those come in handy when the cabdriver's attention is being split between the road and the plate-glass divider full of squeaking pink ass directly over his right shoulder.

2. ON AN AIRPLANE

The mile high club is the ultimate fantasy for everyone who's still stuck in the 1970s and has a limited imagination. If porn is any indication, stewardesses of yore were tall, skanky, and wholly unqualified to do their jobs. Even in the nonporno universe, you're in an exotic place, high above the earth, and sharing close quarters with nothing to do. Who can blame you for getting a little amorous?

Well, the police for starters: You can be arrested for joining the mile high club. There are also the potential safety risks. Plane sex is the only item on this list that combines the reckless risks of having sex in a car with the potential diseases of having sex in a location that's teaming with poop. A twofer!

And we're pretty sure the payoff isn't worth it. Airplane bathrooms aren't famous for their roominess. Joining the mile high club is like having sex in a kitchen cabinet, if your kitchen cabinet has a bunch of faucets and handles inside and an audience of total strangers sitting within earshot of your clumsy, apologetic humping.

Jordan Monsell

1. THE WOODS

Few things are more romantic than packing up for a weekend, heading to the great outdoors, getting a fire going, pitching a tent, and then crawling inside with your honey for some awkward, claustrophobic sex on uneven ground.

Unfortunately, while nature enthusiasts may enjoy the freedom of humping under the stars, park officials say there's some cause for alarm. See, you won't just *look* like two sausages trying to fit in the same casing as you hump away in your sleeping bags. There are parts of the food chain where that shit smells like dinner.

Specifically, the bear part.

Park rangers in bear country caution against having sex for the same reason they caution against dipping a fresh salmon in honey and putting it down your pants. A bear thinks the juices your body produces during sex smell delicious. The better the sex, the more likely that sound you just heard isn't "just the fire settling in for the night."

And while we apologize for how difficult that's going to make it to ever achieve an orgasm in anything even resembling an outdoor setting, why would you want to? While some sex may be worth getting arrested by an air marshal, we're hard pressed to present a single sexual experience on record that's worth a bear attack.

Jordan Monsell

FIVE AWESOME THINGS YOU DIDN'T KNOW COULD MAKE YOU SICK

THANKS to dedicated doctors and researchers, the number of common objects and activities you must fear has multiplied a thousandfold. Every day, medical professionals work toward a humanitarian goal centuries old: to catalog every possible way you can get sick and die.

5. ART

Stendhal syndrome is an "attack of dizziness, confusion, elevated heartbeat, or hallucination upon exposure to great works of art." It was first diagnosed in the nineteenth century, when Stendhal took a trip to Florence and got a face full of aesthetically transcendent disease. Since then, there have been 107 documented sufferers, including Fyodor Dostoevsky.

The diagnosis's stipulation that the art must be great raises a number of troubling and ridiculous questions. Do doctors in the general proximity of the Louvre have a list of the works that qualify as great? Do they throw up their hands in befuddlement when patients fly into seizures at the sight of art the medical establishment deems "pretty good" or "just aight"? Could it be that Stendhal syndrome is simply a snootier version of the syndrome that teenage girls have been suffering from at Michael Jackson and Justin Timberlake concerts for years?

Until more is known, doctors recommend steering clear of anything that has shown even the slightest whiff of cultural value. Or they would if you couldn't also get seizures from . . .

4. MARY HART'S VOICE

Mary Hart's voice has always been known to hold tremendous power. It can determine what passes for tonight's entertainment or sink a budding celebrity romance before it ever gets off the ground. But as recorded in a 1991 *New England Journal of Medicine* article, it can also cause violent epileptic seizures. The article relates the case of a woman who, upon hearing Hart's voice, suffered "an abnormal electrical discharge in the brain, disorientation, nausea, and headaches." She only got the seizures when she watched *Entertainment Tonight*, and they stopped as soon as she switched stations.

Doctors call the syndrome reflex epilepsy, and almost anything can trigger it. People have been known to go into fits after seeing Pokémon cartoons, looking at the logo for the 2012 Olympics, playing Nintendo, or hearing the Sean Paul song "Temperature." Although most doctors agree that the last one was merely an appropriate response to the stimulus.

Anthony Clark

The fact is, you may not even know you *have* reflex epilepsy until you run into your trigger. One minute you're asking the friendly clerk at IKEA how to pronounce the name of the duvet you've just purchased, the next minute you're flopping on the floor trying to swallow your own tongue. The only way to truly be safe is to keep a piece of leather clenched between your teeth at all times.

3. HULA HOOPS

That hula hoop collecting cobwebs in your garage may well be the deadliest plastic circle since the O-rings on the *Challenger*. In 1992, a Beijing man was hospitalized with a twisted intestine after "playing excessively" with a hula hoop. Chinese papers said that the case was the third in a few weeks and blamed it on a hula hoop craze sweeping China at the time. This also represented the first time the phrase "hula hoop craze" had been printed in a newspaper since the thirties.

Fortunately, the Beijing man was treated successfully and eventually able to return to work (presumably deep in an unstable coal mine). Not so lucky was the Korean woman admitted in 2006 for a perirenal hematoma developed after six months of routine "violent hula hooping." In case you don't know what a perirenal hematoma is, that means the hula hoop *made blood come out of her kidneys*. It looks like you're going to have to somehow resist the lure of violently hula hooping for long periods of time.

If you're starting to think that the only way to avoid death is to shut yourself inside your house, don't worry . . .

2. STAYING SAFELY INDOORS

Over the last decade or so, a wide range of seemingly unrelated illnesses have started to be attributed to sick building syndrome, which is basically any disease you get just by being inside. Victims have reported everything from headaches and fatigue to hair loss and neurological problems, all tied to starting work at a new building or moving into a new house. Because their symptoms differ so widely, and because "coming into work makes me sick" sounds like the lamest excuse ever, the disease wasn't even really studied until recently.

The current theory is that newer buildings, which are better insulated than old ones, may be too airtight for their own good, trapping toxic gasses and causing air to stagnate. And that air is filled with all the dust, gas, and molecular detritus left over from the construction process, as well as whatever stray compounds the drying paint and setting concrete decide to contribute. Think of it like a balloon full of poison, except you work inside the balloon, and instead of it being someone's birthday party, your hair is falling out in clumps. Also, most people you tell about your illness call you a crazy liar.

1. THE INTERNET

Telling people about all the things that will make them sick is one of the Web's primary functions. But only since a recent report in *Biologist*, a UK science journal, has it been thought that the Internet could actually suppress your immune system, encourage disease, and speed the growth of tumors. The report cites studies showing that entering the twenty-first century, time spent using electronic media increased, while time spent in actual face-to-face social interaction dropped significantly. This lack of daily human interaction causes your body to slack off and fail to produce as many white blood cells and cytokines (those are good).

While keeping your distance from a bunch of filthy human bacteria might seem like a good thing, your immune system actually needs the activity. After months spent sitting alone, surfing porn, your body's natural defense system begins to atrophy.

So really, it's not the Internet that's making you sick; it's the crushing, crushing loneliness. If you want to stay healthy, don't waste your time reading books or browsing the supremely addictive Cracked.com website. Go out and get some exercise. But before you do that, you might want to turn to the next section to learn about all the ways exercise can kill you too.

FOUR THINGS YOUR MOM SAID WERE HEALTHY THAT CAN KILL YOU

EVERYONE knows that fad diets aren't to be trusted. But there are a few simple rules that seem never to go out of style. Exercise like a madman, hit the four food groups, get eight hours of sleep at night, and avoid stuff that's high in fat. Do all those things and you'll be well on your way to . . . a premature death. Yep, the ABCs of healthy living lead directly to an early grave. And we've known it for years.

4. EXERCISING

Exercise is good for you. Exercise is hard. Therefore the more you exercise, the better off your body will be, right? There's no better example of this line of reasoning than the marathon, which is named for the legendary Greek messenger who ran 26.2 miles from a battle in Marathon to Athens, announced to the general assembly, "We won," and promptly dropped dead.

Ignoring the cautionary-tale shape to that story arc, the modern fitness movement made the recreation of the mythical death sprint their de facto symbol of peak physical condition (the ancient Greco-Roman sports of nude wrestling and lion fighting were presumably dismissed as too gay and too cruel to animals, respectively). And while it's true that only the fit can possibly handle such a distance, it turns out it's not necessarily good for the smug bastards.

Running a marathon is, on balance, bad for your muscles, your immune system, and even your heart. It's so traumatic that your body begins leaking injury-signaling enzymes. In an interview with *Men's Health*, Dr. Arthur Siegel said, "Your body doesn't know whether you've run a marathon . . . or been hit by a truck." Siegel's the director of internal medicine at Harvard's McLean hospital, who ran twenty marathons before he was convinced to hang up his ridiculous short shorts by his research and all the heart attacks he kept seeing at the marathons he ran. Yes, heart attacks. It happens about a dozen times a year. Runners' hearts give out or they go into complete renal failure. After hours of extensive research, we have it on good authority that doing anything to the point that your organs shut down is generally a bad thing.

However, because our culture tends to view exercise as the

physiological equivalent of putting money into your 401(k), marathon runners have been known to ignore their body's "you're goddamned killing us" message until they're doing a horrifyingly faithful recreation of the first marathon ever.

The truth is that, like most things, exercise should be practiced in moderation. As Spiegel advises in the article, you're probably better off training for a marathon and then not running it. Of course, that won't prove to the world that you're a bigger badass than that Greek messenger.

3. HALF OF THE FOUR MAJOR FOOD GROUPS

Back in 1977, Senator George McGovern and the Senate Select Committee on Nutrition (SSCON) were asked to figure out why so many Americans were showing up at hospitals with the muscle definition (and often the heart rates) of a Jell-O casserole. Undertaking the most comprehensive study of American dietary habits in history, the SSCON revealed that, despite America's unwavering commitment to lard-assed heart abuse, rates of obesity, diabetes, and heart disease briefly dipped during World War II. After rigorous lab experiments determined that you couldn't Nazi hunt your way to low cholesterol, the committee arrived at a more practical explanation: meat and dairy rations. America got healthier during WWII because they weren't allowed to eat all the beef and cheese they could fit their mouths around.

Figuring that some self-imposed rationing might do some good, the committee drafted a report that urged Americans to "cut red meat and dairy intake drastically." As bad as that news was for American taste buds, it was worse for cattle farmers. Since 1955, they'd been making obscene amounts of money selling the half of the USDA's "four essential food groups" that contained cheeseburgers and milk shakes. Luckily for future manufacturers of scoop-'n'-eat cheesecake and muumuus, by the time the SSCON released their report, they'd made enough money to hire an army of lobbyists. Soon after releasing the report, committee members were told it would need some revisions if they wanted to keep their jobs.

Doing what politicians do best, the SSCON caved. The clear and direct "reduce consumption of meat" became, "Choose meats, poultry and fish that will reduce saturated-fat intake." To ensure that no other senators got any funny ideas about making Americans skinny, the meat and dairy industries spent millions to ensure McGovern's ass got kicked to the curb in the very next election. American waistlines continued expanding, life spans continued shrinking, and nobody even dreamed of pissing off cattle ranchers ever again.

2. GETTING EIGHT HOURS OF SLEEP EVERY NIGHT

If there's one lie that's ingrained into America's youth even earlier than "drinking milk turns you into a muscle-bound shit wrecker," it's the idea that you need eight hours of sleep each night. The bedtimes of children and the schedules of adults are structured around this one easy-to-remember bodily mandate. For years, it's been dividing weekdays into three convenient eight-hour chunks of work, relaxation, and sleep.

Dr. Daniel Kripke of the University of California, San Diego, conducted a sleep study that tracked adults from the time they were old enough to set their own bedtime to the time they took a permanent nap in the dirt. The study found that seven hours of sleep seems to be the "golden time" for maximum health. Those who got less than seven hours saw slight decreases in life span. The ones who got the magic number

of eight hours? They were, on average, *even worse off.* Despite what your parents told you, Kripke found that eight hours is the duration at which sleep turns from "healthy and relaxing" to "slowest form of suicide imaginable."

Before you start petitioning your local representative to draft laws banning comfortable beds, smooth jazz, and the writing of Immanuel Kant (for the children!), the studies didn't show that seven hours is the perfect length of sleep for everyone. Like anything involving the human brain, sleep is way too complicated for blanket rules. The problem, according to Kripke, is that people who naturally sleep less than eight hours a night think they're not getting enough sleep. That's why sleeping pills do such a robust business despite health risks that he puts on level with smoking cigarettes. People who need less than eight hours think they have to force their bodies across an arbitrary finish line their parents invented.

So the next time you're lying awake in bed, worried that you're now seven hours and forty-eight minutes away from the alarm, just remember, eight hours is just something your parents made up because they wanted some alone time to have filthy sex on the couch where you grew up watching TV.

Or maybe just count sheep.

1. THE GODDAMN FOOD PYRAMID

In 1992, the government decided to take another run at America's rampant ass jigglery, this time designing an official info graphic that showed how many servings of different food groups you should get in a day. Just as the four food groups had improved on 1943's Basic Seven, which actually included *butter* as its own group, the food pyramid took a few steps in the right direction. For instance, it separated fruits and vegetables into their own categories and suggested that both were more essential than the cheese and burger groups. The USDA even created a villain, the tiny tip of the pyramid, fats and oils, which Americans were advised to use sparingly. Having outlined its complex nutritional morality play, the USDA dusted off its hands, sat back, and watched childhood obesity rise every year since.

Again, the government had suffered from a crisis of testicular fortitude. Rather than suggesting that anyone eat less of anything, which could hurt the $500 billion food industry, the pyramid suggested that you eat bad foods less frequently *relative to* how many good foods you eat. It also followed the SSCON's tradition of blaming the word *fats* rather than anything you might recognize from your grocery list. Food manufacturers responded by flooding the market with chips and cookies chemically engineered to be "low in fat," giving Americans the green light to eat their way skinny.

Of course, it wasn't *all* on "the man." The chart gave our

Jordan Monsell

fat asses too much wiggle room. Choosing from the items listed in each section, you could eat three cheeseburgers, down two glasses of OJ, three servings of fries (cooked in McDonald's new low-fat lard!), a box of Lucky Charms, and go to bed telling your body it could thank you on your hundredth birthday.

As for those new chemically engineered low-fat miracle foods, studies show no evidence that they have any effect on heart or overall body health. Eleftheria Maratos-Flier, director of obesity research at Harvard's Joslin Diabetes Center says, "For a large percentage of the population, perhaps 30 to 40 percent, low-fat diets are counterproductive. They have the paradoxical effect of making people gain weight."

Nutritionists hold out hope that we might turn a corner in the next fifteen years though, when the costs of airlifting children to school passes the $500 billion mark.

Winston Rowntree

THE GRUESOME ORIGINS OF FIVE POPULAR FAIRY TALES

FAIRY tales weren't always for kids. Back when these stories were first told in the taverns of medieval villages, there were very few kids present. These were racy, violent parables to distract peasants after a hard day's dirt farming, and some of them made *Hostel* look like, well, kid's stuff.

5. LITTLE RED RIDING HOOD: INTERSPECIES SEX PLAY, CANNIBALISM

The version you know

On her way to her grandmother's, Little Red Riding Hood meets the Big Bad Wolf and stupidly tells him where she's going. He gets there first, eats Grandma, puts on her dress, and waits for Red.

She gets there, they do the back-and-forth about what big teeth he has, and he eats her. Then, a passing woodsman comes and cuts Red and Grandma out of the wolf, saving the day.

What got changed

Like many fairy tales, the modern version of "Little Red Riding Hood" comes from Frenchman Charles Perrault's seventeenth-century Mother Goose tales. While Perrault collected and retold the folktales for children, he wasn't afraid to straight-up kill some bitches to make a point.

The big thing that changed about this one since Perrault's version is the ending. That woodsman showing up seemed a little like a third-act movie rewrite due to bad test screening, didn't it?

In Perrault's version of the story, Red and her grandmother are dead. The. Goddamn. End.

Perrault's was the PG version of the tale he'd probably heard as a boy. According to a collection of oral folktales from the Middle Ages, the earlier versions liked to spice up the sexual undertones, having Red catch on to the wolf and perform a striptease while he's lying in bed dressed as her grandmother before running away while he's "distracted" (note to any young girls: If you are ever abducted and menaced by someone, *do not do this!*).

Wait, it gets worse. In some of the early folktales, the Wolf dissects Grandmother, then invites Red in for a meal of her flesh, Hannibal Lecter–style.

Sweet dreams!

4. SNOW WHITE:
PRINCE PEDOPHILE, MORE CANNIBALISM

The version you know

Evil stepmom hates that her daughter is prettier than her, so she tells one of her men to take her out to the woods, kill her, and bring back her heart as proof. He can't follow through, so he tells her to run away.

Snow White flees and falls in with seven dwarves. The stepmom finds out and sneaks her a poison apple. Snow goes into a coma until a handsome prince rescues her and they live happily ever after.

What got changed

In the Disney film, the wicked stepmother winds up dead, so that's already pretty hard-core. It's got nothing on the German Grimm brothers, who wrote over a hundred years after Perrault and are probably the second most popular source for modern fairy tales. In their version, the stepmother is tortured by being forced to wear red-hot iron shoes and made to dance until she falls down dead.

iron shoes and made to dance until she falls down dead.

The issue of Snow's actual age is a point of contention as well. The Grimms explicitly refer to her as being seven years old when the story starts, and while there's no firm indication of how much time has passed, it can't be more than a couple of years. So unless that's an eight-year-old prince who comes along and rescues Snow, we're backing away from this one.

The biggest thing we cut out of the Grimms' version, and the bloodiest, is the stepmom's unusual eating habits. Namely, when she asks her guy to bring back the heart of Snow White, she isn't just after proof that the girl is dead. She wants to eat it. Depending on the version of the story, the stepmother asks for Snow's liver, lungs, intestines, or pretty much every other major internal organ, up to and including a bottle of Snow's blood stoppered with her toe.

3. RUMPELSTILTSKIN: DISMEMBERMENT, DEAD TODDLERS

The version you know

The king sentences a beautiful woman to be executed in three days unless she can follow through on her father's claim that she can spin straw into gold (the legal system back then took a much harsher stance on ridiculous bullshit). Luckily, a gnome shows up and offers to spin gold in exchange for her firstborn child. She accepts, the gnome spins her gold, and the king is so impressed that he decides to marry her.

The king and his new queen have a son, and the little gnome shows up demanding the boy unless the queen can guess his name in three days. She tries everything but comes up short, until a passing woodsman overhears the gnome bragging about how he's so clever that no one will guess his name is Rumpelstiltskin. The woodsman immediately tells the queen, who springs it on Rumpelstiltskin, who's so pissed off that he throws a tantrum and runs away, presumably to ply his poorly thought-out scam in another town.

What got changed

In the Grimm brothers' version, the little man is so pissed off that he stamps the floor in his little hissy fit and gets stuck. And then he pulls so hard to free himself that he tears himself in half. Now, if our names were Rumpelstiltskin and some pretty girl told the whole damn room, we'd be pissed too, but we don't think we'd get dismemberment-angry.

In the early folktales on which the Grimm version was based, Rumpelstiltskin launches himself at the girl in a rage and gets stuck, um, in her lady parts. Like a gynecological "Humpty Dumpty," the palace guards have to come and pull him out, which must have made for some awkward looks afterward.

Also, in a depressingly large number of the early versions the child is killed anyway, either by Rumpelstiltskin himself or the guards. They weren't big on happy endings in the Dark Ages.

2. SLEEPING BEAUTY: COMA SEX

The version you know

"Sleeping Beauty" is the story of a young princess who is cursed by an evil witch so that she will prick her finger on a spindle and die on her fifteenth birthday. Fortunately, a nonevil old lady finds out and tempers the curse—the princess won't die, she'll just fall asleep for a hundred years.

Of course the king orders all spindles burned, plunging the kingdom into a fashion nightmare, but with the inevitability of fairy-tale logic bearing down on her, the princess manages to find the one working spindle in the kingdom and pricks her finger on her fifteenth birthday. She falls asleep for a hundred years, until a dashing young prince comes along in timely fashion and kisses her, breaking the spell.

What got changed

Seventeenth-century Italian poet and collector of fairy tales Giambattista Basile wrote an early version in which the princess instead gets a piece of flax caught under her fingernail, which puts her to sleep. This might seem like a small difference but stick around.

Basile's version then has the prince who finds the sleeping princess think she's so damn beautiful that he just goes ahead and has his way with her right then and there, while she's still comatose.

If that's not disturbing enough, the Rohypnol-style coupling leads to a pregnancy, and the princess gives birth to twins, all while asleep. One of the babies, seeking Momma's milk, sucks on her finger and dislodges the flax, waking her, at which point we imagine she had a few questions.

1. CINDERELLA: MUTILATION, SEX, MORE MUTILATION

The version you know

You all know it: The stepmother and stepsisters hate beautiful Cinderella and make her work all day. One day a fairy godmother shows up and gives Cinderella pretty clothes and a pumpkin coach and sends her to the ball where she falls in love with the prince.

But at the stroke of midnight it all ends, and she runs home, leaving only her glass slipper behind. The prince searches the land, finds Cinderella, the shoe fits, and they live happily ever after.

What got changed

Everyone seemed to have a version of this one. A famous difference in many of the stories is the glass slipper. Authorities on fairy tales (whom you tend not to see at parties) disagree about whether Perrault's slipper was made of glass or fur, as the words in French (*verre* and *vair*) are pronounced almost identically. It's kind of important, because if the prince was wandering the land looking for a lady with the perfect "fur slipper," well, it doesn't take Freud to figure that one out. Suddenly the prince doesn't look so noble.

One thing Perrault left out that the Grimms delighted in putting back was the violence. The sisters, desperate to fit into the slipper, mutilate their own feet, cutting off their toes and heels in exquisite Germanic detail. When the prince eventually realizes that Cinderella is the one for him, birds peck out the sisters' and mother's eyes for their wickedness.

You can probably understand why Disney went with Perrault's ending for its adaptation.

FIVE HORRIFYING FOOD ADDITIVES YOU'VE PROBABLY EATEN TODAY

DECIPHERING food labels is tricky business. They're filled with lots of multisyllabic words that border on being impossible to pronounce, chemicals that sound like they could kill you just by touching them, and much, much worse. Read on, unless you've eaten recently.

5. SHELLAC

Most everyone is familiar with shellac as a wood-finishing product. It's often used to give furniture, guitars, and even AK-47's that special shine. But did you know that it is also commonly used as a food additive? Yep, that's why those jelly beans you gorge on every Easter are so shiny.

But what exactly is shellac?

Are you sure you want to know?

Shellac is derived from the excretions of an insect, *Kerria lacca*, most commonly found in the forests of Thailand. *Kerria lacca* uses the slime as a means to stick to the trees on which it lives. Candy makers then come along and harvest the *Kerria lacca* excretion by scraping it right off the tree. Unfortunately for you and your future enjoyment of shiny candies, this leaves little room for quality control measures to guarantee that the insects aren't scooped up as well.

Once that happens, and it almost always does, the insects simply become part of the shellac-making process. And the candy-making process. And the candy-eating process.

Don't eat candy? That's OK: You're probably eating bugs too. During the cleaning process, apples lose their natural shine. Care to guess how it's restored?

If all of this is making you a bit queasy, we understand. It's not every day that you find out you've been celebrating the resurrection of Jesus by consuming handfuls of insect-infused treats your entire life. But before you head to the medicine cabinet, consider this. That pill you want to take to quell your nausea? It didn't get shiny on its own.

4. BONE CHAR

The sugar you put on your cereal in the morning didn't start out white. It's naturally brown—a color the food industry apparently decided was undesirable. To make their product more acceptable to whitey, sugar companies use a filtering process to strip it of its color. In some cases, the process involves boring sciency words like *ions* and such. But sugar derived from sugarcane (about a quarter of the sugar in the United States) goes through a . . . different process.

Domino, the largest sugar producer in America, uses something called bone char to filter impurities from its sugar. Bone char is produced using the bones of cows from India, Pakistan, and Afghanistan that have died from "natural causes," as opposed to cows who forget to wear a helmet when riding their motorcycles.

The bones are bleached in the sun and sold to marketers who then sell them to the U.S. sugar industry. Sugar companies then heat the bones until charred, at which point they are used to filter the sugar that keeps you fat and happy.

We don't know by what alchemy this method purifies the sugar, but since they go out of their way to use ground-up cow bones from India—a country where that animal is often considered sacred—we have to assume Satan is involved.

3. CARMINE

Carmine can also be identified on food labels as crimson lake, cochineal, Natural Red 4, CI 75470, or E120. We mention that because we're guessing you'll want to check for it after reading this.

If you're eating something red right now, or have recently, you're probably eating carmine, which is ground-up cochineal insects—essentially mashed red beetles. Because you're dying to know more, the insects are killed by exposure to heat or immersion in hot water and then dried. Because the female abdominal region that houses the fertilized eggs contains the most carmine, it is separated from the rest of the body, ground into a powder, and cooked at high temperatures to extract the maximum amount of color.

Then it's added to that yogurt you ate this morning while lording your health consciousness over the guy in the cubicle next to you who had an Egg McMuffin.

Food manufacturers are well aware that word has gotten out about exactly what carmine is and that people are less than crazy about it. So a number of crafty manufacturers have resorted to labeling it not as carmine but instead as "natural color," thereby guaranteeing you'll never really know for sure if your cherry ice cream contains the USDA recommended amount of creepy crawlers.

Hey, speaking of that . . .

2. NATURAL FLAVOR

When it comes to food, most of us get nervous when people are intentionally vague. We steer clear of the street vendor selling "meat soup" and "food burritos."

So when you see that a label has included "natural flavor," you should be equally alarmed. If you're thinking the natural flavor in your orange candy must have come from oranges, think again. If it was from oranges, they would say so right on the can. It would be a selling point.

The problem is, natural flavor can be anything that isn't

man-made. Cat urine could be a natural flavor. If someone discovered that goat jizz added a special zing to ice cream and they could prove that eating it wouldn't make you sick: natural flavor. And because they know people would rather see the word *natural* on the label than some fancy-pants chemical compound, it's actually in their interest to go with the goat jizz.

Vitamin A 0%   Vitamin C 0%
Calcium 0%   Iron 0%
*Percent Daily Values are based on a 2,000 calorie diet.

INGREDIENTS: Natural Flavor, Bits of Food, Taste Parts, Nutrition, Perfectly Normal Additives, Nothing Weird, Ordinary Stuff, Absolutely Unremarkable Components

ALLERGY WARNING: Processed in a factory that also processes spiders.

Anthony Clark

One potentially disturbing example of natural flavor gone bad comes from—where else?—McDonald's. Back in 1990, amid constant public outcry about the amount of cholesterol in its french fries, McDonald's started using pure vegetable oil in its fryers.

Wait, what were they using before? Why, beef lard. When they stopped using it, and McDonald's realized that fried potatoes don't taste as good without some molten beef added, it was "natural flavor" to the rescue.

When vegetarian groups demanded to know what the mystery flavor was, company reps would only say it was "animal derived."

They wouldn't say what animal. According to the book *Fast Food Nation*, "Beef is the probable source, although other meats cannot be ruled out. In France, for example, fries are sometimes cooked in duck fat or horse tallow." Now, we all know how uptight French people are about their food. If their fries are being boiled in the processed knee joints of Kentucky

Derby hopefuls, what does that mean for us Americans? Use your imagination.

1. BACTERIOPHAGES

In 2006, the FDA approved the use of bacteriophages to fight *Listeria* microbes on lunch meat, wieners, and sausages. If you're unfamiliar with the term *bacteriophages*, let us put it in a layman's term for you: viruses.

In this case, six viruses, to be exact. There is an excellent chance that ham sandwich you had for lunch this afternoon was sprayed with a mixture of six different viruses in an effort to fight a microbe that kills hundreds of people a year. Hundreds. Approximately the same number of people that die in plane crashes. Because of this clear and present danger, your lunch meat is slathered with an array of viruses.

This probably sounds bad enough already, but wait until you hear Intralytix, the company that developed the bacteriophage mixture, explain exactly how the virus works. "Typical phages have hollow heads that store their viral DNA and tunnel tails with tips that bind to specific molecules on the surface of their target bacteria. The viral DNA is injected through the tail into the host cell, where it directs the production of progeny phages."

We'll take it from here. The battlefield on which this virus-versus-microbe war plays out is the bologna that you used to prepare your afternoon lunch. Around the same time the hollow-headed bacteriophages were storming the beach at *Listeria*, you were lifting that bologna sandwich to your mouth. Just as the phages were thrusting their hollow, viral-DNA-filled tails into the host cells (also living on your sandwich), you were jamming the whole nasty battle right down your oblivious gullet.

If you've ever tried the Subway diet without success, this might be a good time to give it another shot. If thinking about the rampant virus-versus-microbe violence you're about to ingest doesn't put you off eating for the rest of the day, then nothing will, tubby.

Winston Rowntree

FIVE STORIES THE MEDIA DOESN'T WANT YOU TO KNOW ABOUT

AT its best, the media is a knife at the throat of tyrants every-where, the ever-watchful guardian of the interests of the peo-ple. Unfortunately, it's rarely at its best—hell, you're lucky if it puts on pants in the morning. More often than not it's, uh . . . this.

5. *USA TODAY*'S STAR REPORTER LIES TO THE PUBLIC . . . FOR TWENTY-ONE YEARS

When It Happened: 1991–2004

News Agencies Involved: *USA Today*

Back in 2004, *USA Today* was the most widely read newspaper in the United States, and its star reporter was Jack Kelley, a Pulitzer Prize–winning twenty-one-year newspaper veteran notorious for getting impossible scoops. He wrote gripping first-person accounts of riding with Army Special Forces to catch bin Laden; watching a Pakistani student unfold a picture of the Sears Tower and say, "This one is mine," in 2001; and infiltrating bands of terrorists around the world. He was like Jack Bauer, only with a pen instead of a pistol (and judging from Bauer having never *once* moved his bowels in 192 hours of screen time, equally full of shit).

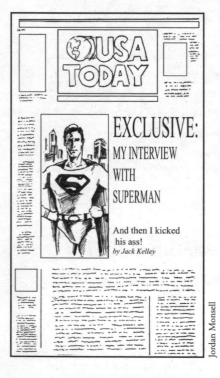

Over twenty-one years of professional bullshitting, whenever a colleague would raise a question about Kelley's latest scoop, "Jack Kelley Revealed to Have Largest Penis Ever," they were shot down by the editors. Eventually, someone filed a complaint that stuck. When the higher-ups asked to speak to a translator Kelley used on a story, Kelley handed one of his friends a script and asked her to pretend to be the woman in question. Somehow this didn't work out (it was probably his insistence that she pepper her responses with flattering anecdotes about his mastery of karate sutra, the deadly art of sex-fighting). When *USA Today* launched an investigation, it found Kelley had made up "all or part of 20 stories that appeared in the paper, lifted more than 100 passages and quotes from other, uncredited sources." There was no Pakistani student gunning for the Sears Tower, and he never infiltrated anything or rode along on a hunt for bin Laden. And then there was his heartrending tale, in 2000, of a Cuban woman who died trying to flee her country by boat. Turned out the woman in the snapshot he provided the editors was a Cuban hotel worker who they tracked down in 2004, alive and well.

What it taught us about the media

You could walk into a major newspaper, introduce yourself as Jack Ryan, and hand in an excerpt of a Tom Clancy novel. They'd put in the next morning's paper. Then they'd win the Pulitzer.

4. THE GREAT MOON HOAX

When It Happened: 1835

News Agencies Involved: *The New York Sun*

In 1835, the *New York Sun* duped the people of the United States into believing that aliens had been discovered on the moon.

To its credit, it attributed this fantastic discovery to John

Herschel, the best-known astronomer of his day. Herschel was the perfect cover because he was famous yet reclusive. Since telephones hadn't been invented, it was virtually impossible for Herschel to dispute the *Sun*'s claims, and the ridiculous scheme worked: The *Sun* increased its subscriber base by over fifteen thousand daily after the first story.

Having learned a valuable lesson about deceiving its readers (specifically, hey this shit works!) the *Sun* announced the life that was discovered on the moon consisted of intelligent batmen. Once again, circulation increased, making the *Sun* the largest newspaper on the planet. The story was so thoroughly believed that a Springfield, Massachusetts, missionary society resolved to send missionaries to the moon to convert and civilize the bat-men, apparently unaware that bat-men have lost all faith since they saw their parents gunned down in that alleyway.

What it taught us about the media

The story was revealed to be a hoax several weeks after its publication, but since there was no television or radio, the news didn't spread very far. The *Sun* never had to issue a retraction, and its circulation didn't decrease as a result. Nevertheless, the media learned its lesson: Don't tell falsehoods unless you like giant piles of money that will last forever with no repercussions.

3. MICHAEL BAY DIRECTS THE NEWS

In 1992, *Dateline NBC* aired an investigative report that showed unsettling videos of GM pickup trucks exploding on impact in low-speed collisions, presumably due to faulty fuel tanks . . . or wizards.

Harry Pearce, GM's executive vice president at the time, attempted to discredit the story with a press conference that involved what legal scholars call "a shitload of evidence." During the press conference, Pearce produced a letter NBC sent him claiming the vehicles used in the video had been "junked" and, as a result, couldn't be inspected. Then he produced the astonishingly not-junked cars. Before the folks at *Dateline* could respond, "Oh, you wanted the *cars we used in the footage!* We thought you said *cards*, and we were like, 'huh?' Ah, but no, the cars are fine . . . ," Pearce was ready to move on to act 2 of *Ruining NBC's Shit: The Reckoning*.

Next, he brought out a blown-up screen grab of the collision that NBC aired and zoomed in on two tiny plumes of smoke coming out of the side of the pickup truck. The problem with this was that the screen grab was taken just moments *before* impact. The GM pickup truck explosion that aired on the NBC program was actually caused by NBC. The producers had rigged the trucks prior to filming. There was literally a guy standing off camera pushing a button a split second before the filmed impact.

Of the five people responsible for the report, three were fired, one resigned, and one got transferred faster than a touch-y priest.

What it taught us about the media
We at Cracked.com like to think the best about people, so the only explanation is that the *Dateline* producers were drunk. For weeks. And GM was holding one of their daughters hostage.

2. EVERY MEDIA NETWORK IN THE COUNTRY STICKS ITS FINGERS IN IS EARS AND SHOUTS, "NAH NAH NAH, I CAN'T HEAR YOU"

When It Happened: 2009

News Agencies Involved: ABC, CBS, NBC, MSNBC, CNN, Fox

In 2008, *New York Times* journalist David Barstow discovered that in the run-up to the Iraq War, every single major media outlet had featured pro-war "impartial experts" who were in fact government sock puppets (metaphorically speaking, in all but the most retarded cases). The report even went on to reveal which Pentagon officials' bony wrists were protruding from the asses of which talking heads (still metaphorically speaking . . . hopefully).

In the end, Barstow's report revealed that when it came to the Iraq War America got news that was as reliable as a Chinese Google search for "Tiananmen Square." The Pentagon and major TV news outlets misled Americans into war. That's the information age's Watergate! So why had we never seen Barstow's name before our research intern told us to type it up there?

It turns out the reports, though impossible to deny, were remarkably easy for TV news outlets to ignore, despite the fact that they were published on the front page of the *New York* goddamned *Times*. When Barstow won the Pulitzer Prize for Investigative Reporting in 2009, most television pundits were busy hyping swine flu. Brian Williams had the balls to report that the paper had won five Pulitzers, and even mentioned the subject of three of the stories they'd won for. He just chose not to mention the one they got for pointing out that he's a government stooge.

What it taught us about the media

Hey, those celebrity vaginas aren't going to expose *themselves*. OK, they are, but that's beside the point. The system's not perfect, but it's not Stalinist Russia either. As long as the *New York Times* is around, we have nothing to worry abou— Oh, hey, look. There's one more entry on this list.

1. THE DENIAL OF THE HOLODOMOR

When It Happened: 1932–33

News Agencies Involved: *New York Times*, *International Herald Tribune*, and the *Nation*

When the harvest of 1932 was poorer than expected in most regions of the Soviet Union, it became pretty clear that there wasn't enough food for the Russian people. Unfortunately, Stalin's government was busy convincing the world that Communism was rad, and alerting the world to an impending disaster wasn't part of the PR plan.

Luckily, America had its best Russian reporter on the ground at the time: Walter Duranty, a Pulitzer Prize winner who had interviewed Stalin himself. As millions of Russians began starving

Jordan Monsell

to death and Stalin continued itching his balls indifferently, the *New York Times*' Duranty stepped up to the plate, informing the world:

"Any report of a famine in Russia is today an exaggeration or malignant propaganda. There is no actual starvation or deaths from starvation, but there is widespread mortality from diseases due to malnutrition." The people, you see, weren't starving to death; they were just *dying of malnutrition*. Wait, what the hell?

It turns out that most writers who got approval to enter the Soviet Union were too terrified of Stalin to talk about what was really happening. They pretty much just reported whatever the Soviet government told them to. In Duranty's case, scoring an interview with the year's hottest dictator came with a price. Namely, not alerting the world that 10 million people were about to starve to death.

What it taught us about the media
Everything you've ever read is a lie. Trust no one.

FOUR BRAINWASHING TECHNIQUES
THEY'RE USING ON YOU RIGHT NOW

BRAINWASHING doesn't take a lot of sci-fi gadgetry. There are all sorts of tried-and-true techniques that anyone can use to bypass the thinking part of your brain and flip a switch deep inside that says "OBEY."

In fact, there's an entire arsenal of manipulation techniques being used on you every day to do just that. Techniques like:

4. CHANTING SLOGANS

Every cult leader, drill sergeant, and politician knows that if you want to quiet all of those pesky doubting thoughts in a crowd, get them to scream a repetitive phrase or slogan. You know it as chanting, but at New York City's Cult Hotline and Clinic, the practice is known as a thought-stopping technique. Guess why.

Why it works

The analytical parts of your brain and those that handle repetitive tasks just can't seem to function at the same time.

In a 2000 *New Yorker* article, Malcolm Gladwell argued that this is why athletes choke in big moments. The heightened pressure turns on the analytical part of their brain while they're trying to complete a repetitive task. Athletes refer to this as "overthinking a shot," or "pooping the wedding bed."

Chanting just reverses the dynamic. It forces your brain into repetitive-task mode so you can't think rationally. For instance, try solving a complex logic puzzle while screaming the chorus to that "I get knocked down" song over and over again.

Meditation works the same way, with chants or mantras meant to "calm the mind." Shutting down those nagging voices in the head is helpful for stressed-out individuals but even more helpful to a guy who wants to shut down an audience full of nagging voices suggesting that what he's saying might be ridiculous.

3. SLIPPING BULLSHIT INTO YOUR SUBCONSCIOUS

The rise of the Internet has given birth to a whole new, sly technique of bullshit insertion. People who get paid to manipulate your opinion have figured out that most of us browse headlines instead of actually reading the news. And there's a way to exploit that based on how the brain stores memories.

The Drudge Report lives off this. A single anonymous source will report to a news blog that, say, Senator Smith runs a secret gay bordello. Drudge will run the headline:

> NEW QUESTIONS ABOUT SMITH'S SECRET GAY BORDELLO

Or perhaps there'll just be a question mark on the end:

> SMITH: SECRET GAY BORDELLO ASS MASTER?

Val Gallardo

It doesn't matter that the headline merely involves "questions" about the bordello. The idea has been planted, and two months later when somebody mentions Senator Smith around the water cooler you'll say, "The gay bordello guy, right?"

Why it works

It's called *source amnesia*. According to a 2008 article in the *New York Times*, it's the reason why "you know that the capital of California is Sacramento, but you probably don't remember how you learned it." The brain has limited storage, so it stores just the important nugget but usually discards the trivial context, such as when and where you learned about it.

In the era of information overload, that's a mechanism that can be easily exploited. A piece of information can be presented with all sorts of qualifiers, but often the brain will only remember the ugly rumor and completely forget the qualifiers. It happens even if the headline we read was *specifically* about the rumor being untrue.

You'll see this every election cycle. The entire point of putting a shaky rumor into the press is to force your opponent to deny it, because denial works just as well as the accusation to secure the rumor in the brains of voters. Thanks to source amnesia, for millions of people all three of these:

Smith Denies Gay Bordello Rumors

Smith Refuses Comment on Gay Bordello Rumors

Smith Admits Starting, Visiting, Burning Down Bordello-Orphanage

register as the exact same headline.

2. CONTROLLING WHAT YOU WATCH AND READ

Restriction of reading material is common to every cult. The idea is to insulate the members from any opposing points of view. That's why the guys claiming to be sex messiahs tend to start their polygamous compounds out in the middle of the desert. Not a lot of dissenting voices out there.

It turns out that technique works just as well out in the real world. Only nobody has to drag you into the desert and tell you what to read. Your brain handles that part for them.

Why it works

Our brain is wired to get a quick high from reading things that agree with our own point of view. Scientists at Emory University actually hooked scanners up to the brains of staunch conservatives and liberals and asked them about politically divisive issues. The scans showed the brain's pleasure center lit up when people heard something they agreed with and lit up again when intentionally dismissing information that they disagreed with. Yes, our brain rewards us for being closed-minded dicks.

This is why the Right and Left each has its own publishing arm, and why each one's favorite topic of discussion is how corrupt and ridiculous the other side's media is. Most of us will gladly close ourselves in whichever echo chamber of talk radio, blogs, and cable news outlets give us that little "I *knew it!*" high.

1. KEEPING YOU IN LINE WITH SHAME

You can win any formal debate in college by using our patented technique of simply repeating your opponent's argument in a high-pitched, mocking tone while wiggling your fingers in the air. There really is no defense.

They call this the *appeal to ridicule fallacy*. To which we would reply, "Ooh, appeal to ridicule fallacy! Well, I've got a *phallus* you can *see* right here, college boy."

Professionals have more sophisticated methods, but they still know that if they can portray an idea as ridiculous, the listener usually won't bother examining it any closer to find out if the ridicule is justified.

For instance, the UN recently released a report that found more greenhouse gasses come from cattle than the tailpipes of cars. Luckily for whichever side of the global-warming debate that information pisses off, this statistic can also be stated thusly: "So now they're telling us that—get this—global warming is caused by cows farting! Priceless!"

And now it's ridiculous. Why even consider a piece of information that ridiculous? That's only something a ridiculous person would do! And you're not ridiculous, are you?

Why it works

There are these primitive, lower parts of your brain called amygdalae that control base, emotional reactions. That's where things like contempt and shame come from, and stimulating the amygdalae can completely shut down the analytical part of your brain. The gang calls you a coward, and the next thing you know you're wedging a Roman candle between your butt cheeks.

You can thank evolution for that. Mockery developed as a conformity enforcer, to keep people in line. Way back when humans started forming groups and tribes, social status was everything. Making a person, idea, or behavior the target of mockery gave it a lower social position. If you were associated with the idea, you were left out of the hunting/eating/orgies that made life worthwhile. Thousands of years later, a good dose of mockery can still shut down critical thinking and make us fall right in line.

"The fast, easy way to get tight abs while sticking it to The Man!"

WARNING: consult a doctor before any fitness regimen, especially a life of dereliction and bare-knuckle brawling in a dive bar's basement.

Brendan McGinley

FIVE HOLLYWOOD ADAPTATIONS THAT TOTALLY MISSED THE POINT

AH, publishing a book. It's like getting confirmation that your time here on earth mattered, but putting your thoughts down on paper doesn't come without risks. There's always the chance that Hollywood will turn your book into a movie, and—spoiler alert—*the studio has a few ideas about the ending.* This is showbiz slang for, "We're going to make your story say exactly the opposite of what you'd intended."

5. *FIGHT CLUB*, ALLEGEDLY BASED ON THE BOOK BY CHUCK PALAHNIUK

In rebellion against the shallowness of modern life and IKEA, the narrator creates an imaginary split personality named Tyler Durden, who urges men to beat the crap out of each other and commit random acts of anarchy. As the story reaches a climax, the narrator realizes he needs to rid himself of Tyler and shoots himself in the head, because that's where your imagination lives.

The book ending

The book makes the dubious claim that being shot in the head puts you in the hospital, and that's where we find the narrator. The narrator describes the hospital in beatific language, calling the attendants "angels." But alas, one of the "angels" is a Fight Club member, who ends the book saying, "We look forward to getting you back." Thus we learn that the narrator has created a monster in the Fight Club anarchist group that is out of his control.

Moral of the book

Modern life is emasculating and can provoke a violent backlash by those feeling disconnected from humanity. *This is a bad thing.*

The Hollywood ending

After shooting himself in the head, the narrator naturally has sustained only a minor flesh wound. The film ends with him holding hands with his love interest while watching a massive spectacle take place in the background, which we all recognize as Hollywood shorthand for "everything is going to turn out all right." For those who don't get it, Edward Norton helpfully states, "Everything's going to be fine."

And so ends an uplifting tale of a guy who got out of a rut with a series of violent escapades learned his lesson about taking it too far, and is going to continue with life the better for his experience. Someday he will look back and tell his grandkids this funny story about how he and grandma met, and then pit them against each other in combat.

Moral of the movie

Same as the book but without the consequences. It's not totally surprising, then, that teens across the world started creating *their own fight clubs*, apparently mistaking the movie for an instructional video on how to achieve six-pack abs.

4. *THE MAN IN THE IRON MASK*, ALLEGEDLY BASED ON THE BOOK BY ALEXANDRE DUMAS

The man in the title is Philippe, identical twin of King Louis XIV of France. As often happens with twins, Philippe is good and Louis is evil. Philippe has been imprisoned for most of his life due to his dangerous potential claim to the throne. A group of musketeers finds him and hatches a plan to swap him out by making a dramatic charge down a prison hallway into a point-blank hail of gunfire. At this point in a story about the end of an era of heroes, as the aged, formally retired musketeers are making a brave suicide charge for a just cause, you would expect the heroes to die heroically . . .

The book ending

. . . which is basically what happens in the novel you read in school, though it probably took longer than you expected.

When the musketeers are eventually defeated, Louis puts Philippe away for life and goes down in history as a great king. Thus we learn a sad truth about the human condition: History is written by the winners and the winners are often dickbags.

Moral of the book
The age of chivalry is passing because men of honor are at a natural disadvantage in our modern, amoral world.

The Hollywood ending
As the smoke clears, the firing squad looks into the haze and sees the musketeers completely untouched, striding forward. Moved to tears, the guards put aside their guns and join the musketeers in putting Louis away and proclaiming Philippe king.

The epilogue proclaims that the good Philippe replaced the evil Louis XIV and was the best king of France ever, thus raising a big cheerful middle finger to everything we know about French history.

Moral of the movie
In a world where the age of chivalry is passing, *three men must risk everything*, which is cool because the good guys always win, especially when they're fighting for a cause as handsome as Leonardo DiCaprio. Bonus moral: Hollywood proves that history can be *rewritten* by dickbags too.

3. *FRANKENSTEIN* (1931), ALLEGEDLY BASED ON THE BOOK BY MARY SHELLEY

Dr. Frankenstein decides to fool around in God's domain by creating life from inanimate matter. When this results in a monster, he realizes he's made a mistake and should probably kill it. Disagreeing, the monster fights back and eventually threatens to murder Frankenstein's new wife.

The book ending

Mary Shelley's beast is a monster of his word and kills Frankenstein's wife. Frankenstein's father then dies of grief. Somewhere along the line, his brother, best friend, and trusted family servant also die. Frankenstein ends up chasing the monster to the North Pole, fueled by grief and revenge, and dies of illness just as the monster bursts into his room, makes a speech about how woeful his lot is, and runs off to commit suicide. Everybody learns a lesson about playing God, or they would have if they weren't all dead.

Moral of the book

When man decides to play God, he provokes His wrath.

The Hollywood ending

Frankenstein enlists the help of a good old angry mob to finish off the monster before he can hurt his wife. The film ends with Frankenstein's dad raising a toast to the happy couple and a future grandchild. Sure, Frankenstein messed up with the brain part of his monster, but it's pretty unfair to say it's inherently wrong to reanimate a living sentient being from spare body parts or anything like that. There's no reason he couldn't try again, as long as he's got the old monster-killing squad handy.

Moral of the movie

You can play God, just clean up after yourself.

2. *THE RUNNING MAN,* ALLEGEDLY BASED ON THE BOOK BY STEPHEN KING

Ben Richards is a contestant in a deadly reality show in which he gets money if he can outrun people trying to hunt him, and gets killed if he can't.

The book ending

At the end of Stephen King's book, Richards has almost succeeded in running out the clock, when he gets a call from Killian, the man behind the *Running Man* show. It's a job offer to be the show's lead hunter. The bad news? Richards's wife and daughter were murdered shortly after he started running. Overcome by grief and unhappy at himself for participating in this exploitative system, Killian crashes into the headquarters of the game company, blowing it up and killing himself.

Moral of the book

A prescient message about the ghoulish nature of reality TV and more generally about human nature's love of spectator sports.

The Hollywood ending

Arnold Schwarzenegger straps Killian to a rocket sled and catapults him through a giant neon sign. He makes a bad pun, gets the girl, and walks away into the futuristic sunset as the audience cheers. Nothing is said about whether the company continues to make reality shows where people are killed, but why wouldn't they? That shit was *amazing!*

Moral of the movie
Reality shows are like regular game shows multiplied by awesome.

1. *BRAM STOKER'S DRACULA*, ALLEGEDLY BASED ON THE BOOK BY BRAM STOKER

The vampire Dracula comes to London, where he kills people and turns the innocent Lucy Westenra into a vampire. A ragtag team including Lucy's best friend Mina and Dr. Van Helsing are forced to kill the now vampirized Lucy and then turn their attention toward finishing off Dracula . . .

The book ending
. . . which they do, through teamwork and courage.

Moral of the book
The ancient and unknown things of this world are scary, dark, and powerful. Once unleashed, you will have to do horrific things to make anything right again, such as murdering your own best friend.

The Hollywood ending
After the count trades mortal blows with one of the vampire hunters, Mina *saves him*. It turns out she's the reincarnation of his dead wife and needs to take him to the castle chapel to kiss him, so she can redeem his soul and allow him to ascend to heaven in a beautiful scene. While she's doing that, another one of her friends dies from Dracula wounds, but he wasn't in love with anybody so it's not important. The important thing is that the guy who killed him and turned her best friend into a monster gets to be with his dead wife in heaven.

Moral of the movie

Love never dies and also doesn't sweat the small stuff like *killing innocent people.* Good thing Hollywood got that one out of its system.

Oh, right.

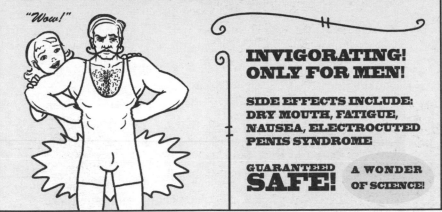

Ben Driscoll

THE TEN MOST INSANE MEDICAL PRACTICES IN HISTORY

DOCTORS have a long, storied background of not knowing what the hell they're doing. History is filled with stories of medical ineptitude, and in all likeliness today's medical practices will be similarly snorted at a hundred years down the road. So if you're looking to rationalize not getting that lump on your neck checked out, you're in the right place.

10. CHILDREN'S SOOTHING SYRUPS

In the nineteenth century, people were simply too busy churning butter and waxing their mustaches to be bothered with disobedient children. To remedy this, a series of "soothing syrups," lozenges, and powders were created, all of which were carefully formulated to ensure they were safe for use by those most vulnerable members of the family. Oh, wait, no. Actually, they pumped each bottle full of as many narcotics as it could hold.

Winston Rowntree

For instance, each ounce of Mrs. Winslow's Soothing Syrup contained sixty-five milligrams of pure morphine.

Based on our experiences experimenting with pure morphine, that seems like a lot. Drug manufacturers finally slowed their roll a bit in 1910, when the *New York Times* decided the whole narcotic babysitter concept was probably bad and ran an article pointing out that these syrups contained, "morphine sulphate, chloroform, morphine hydrochloride, codeine, heroin, powdered opium, cannabis indica," and sometimes several of them in combination.

You can't say the syrups weren't effective, as long as you didn't mind your toddler being strung out on the midnight oil. Or dead. The terrible twos weren't just a cutesy euphemism back then. Kids were not only at their brattiest but also often died, in many cases after their parents tried to cure the aforementioned brattiness with narcotic concoctions in accordance with the doctor's orders.

9. CALM YOUR COUGH WITH HEROIN

Hard drugs weren't just for infants. In the late nineteenth century, people apparently took cough suppression seriously. We're talking, "I'm going to take me some heroin to calm this cough" level serious, here. We know Victorians were sticklers for social etiquette and wheezing your head off was probably considered frightfully rude, but we can't imagine tying off and shooting some horse in the middle of a dinner party would go over terribly well, either.

You probably don't need us to tell you how addictive and destructive heroin is, but just in case: Heroin? Might want to avoid that stuff. On the upside, it actually does suppress coughs, so if you do become a junkie at least you'll save on buying Halls.

Heroin, by the way, was originally developed by Bayer. You know, those friendly folks behind harmless old aspirin. How is that not at the center of every single Tylenol campaign? Tylenol: The fast-acting pain reliever that didn't invent heroin.

8. THE CURATIVE POWERS OF MERCURY

For centuries, mercury was used to treat pretty much everything. Scraped your knee? Just rub a little mercury on it. Having some problems with regularity? Forget fiber, get some mercury up in there! If you lived more than a hundred years ago, you simply weren't considered healthy if you weren't leaking silver from at least one orifice.

Mercury, as we know, is toxic as hell. Symptoms of mercury poisoning include chest pains, heart and lung problems, coughing, tremors, violent muscle spasms, psychotic reactions, delirium, hallucinations, suicidal tendencies, restless spleen syndrome, penis knotting, and anal implosion. OK, we just made the last few up, but they barely looked out of place in that horror show of symptoms, right?

7. ELECTRICAL IMPOTENCE CURES

Men have been desperately trying to fix their malfunctioning members since well before the late nineteenth century, but that's when impotent men discovered the wonders of electricity.

Electrified beds, elaborate cock-shocking electric belts, and other devices were advertised as being able to return "male power" and prowess by making your penis rise to electrified attention like a six-inch-tall Frankenstein's monster.

What's fascinating is that you can find ads for more than one brand of electric dick-shock belt, which seems to indicate that the dick-shock belt industry somehow survived the negative word of mouth from the first dick-shock belt. It would also suggest that the following conversation took place on a regular basis, "What's it do, Doc? Actually, don't answer that, I'm puttin' it on my junk."

6. LOBOTOMIES

You're sitting on your psychiatrist's couch, pouring your tortured heart out about how depressed you are. "I think I have the solution to your depression," he says, producing a ten-inch-long ice pick. "I'm going to jam this into your eye socket, then put it into your brain using this mallet. Then I'll wiggle it around so that it shreds part of your brain. Then you won't be depressed anymore. I'm a doctor."

Congratulations hypothetical 1940s version of yourself, you've just been lobotomized! Lobotomies were a popular fad for the first half of the twentieth century and were floated as a "cure" for pretty much any mental issue you can name, from anxiety to schizophrenia.

The inventor of the lobotomy was given a Nobel Prize for it in 1949. Doctors claimed the ice-pick-to-the-freaking-eye method of lobotomy would be as quick and easy as a trip to the dentist. By 1960, parents were getting them for their moody teenage children.

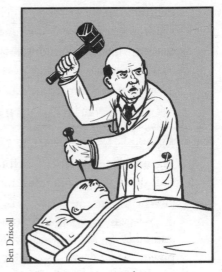

Ben Driscoll

"As you can see, gentlemen, we now know everything there is to know about the human body. I am, like, 95% sure."

In 2005, NPR profiled Howard Dully, a grown man who'd had the procedure performed in 1960, when he was just twelve. Medical records indicate that his stepmother's psychiatrist recommended a lobotomy after she'd complained that he was "defiant," "didn't respond well to punishment," and "objects to going to bed," or as it's known to modern doctors, being a normal freaking twelve-year-old boy.

Some seventy thousand people were lobotomized before somebody figured out that driving a spike into the brain probably was not the answer to all of life's problems.

5. TREPANATION

Like the lobotomy's old, senile grandfather, trepanation is basically a fancy word for drilling holes in your head. It's also the
oldest surgical procedure known to man. Trepanation holes
were found in 40 of 120 human skulls discovered at a prehistoric burial site in France estimated to be eight thousand
years old.

Most commonly used as a treatment for seizures and mi-
graines in the Middle Ages and the Renaissance, it was also
used as an extreme form of cosmetic/experimental body modi-
fication amongst several pre-Columbian American societies.
Nobody's quite sure why the French cavemen did it. Probably
because they'd just invented tools and nobody'd invented any
furniture for them to put together yet.

4. URINE THERAPY

You can tell by the title of this entry that we're not heading
anywhere good. Throughout history there have been those
who believed the key to good health was wallowing in one's
own excretions. Urine was said to cure an endless list of ailments and to promote good health if consumed, was applied
to the skin and, yes, some even used it to give themselves (turn
away now weak of heart) a nice bracing urine enema.

Perhaps the best part of this is that, unlike the other practices listed here, urine therapy lives on today. Of all the crack-
pot theories listed here, the one that endured is the one where
people drink and bathe in piss.

There's absolutely no evidence that urine therapy can cure
a damn thing, though there is conclusive evidence proving
that it can absolutely make you smell like old people.

3. BLOODLETTING

Bloodletting was one of the most enduring and popular medical practices in history, originated by the Greeks and used up until the nineteenth century for, well, basically everything. If you were feeling under the weather back in the day, there's a good chance it was because you just had too much blood.

A person having too much blood may sound absurd, but that's just because you don't know about the four humors. The theory was that the body was filled with blood, phlegm, yellow bile, and black bile and that an imbalance of the four fluids was the root of all illness. Apparently, blood could be a bit of a space hog, and thus patients were bled to make room for more fun stuff like black bile (diarrhea).

If you're wondering what made people think this worked for so long, the next time you're at death's door with the flu go out and give up to four quarts of blood. We can assure you your flu won't be cured, but you'll probably *feel* a lot better as you take a delirious blood-loss-inspired trip through the clouds!

2. HARD-CORE DIET REMEDIES

While fuller figures have been popular for most of history, during the twentieth—or "no fat chicks"—century, thin was in for women. This need to be slim led to the creation of countless so-called diet pills.

While a lot of the pills actually did help with weight loss, they also caused fevers, heart troubles, blindness, death, and birth defects. In the 1950s and 1960s, women liked diet pills so darn much that they just couldn't seem to stop taking them. This was because the diet pills of the '50s and '60s were in actuality bottles of pure crank. But hey, what's being a nervous, amphetamine-addicted wreck when being ready for bathing suit season hangs in the balance?

1. FEMALE HYSTERIA CURES

Women and their mood swings—right, guys? Now, if you happen to be female don't be offended, there's no shame in admitting to the occasional bit of moodiness (or irritability or anxiousness or a ton of other things) as according to nineteenth-century doctors it's a symptom of a deadly serious medical condition.

So how do you cure a "condition" that coincidentally was diagnosed almost entirely in women who dared disobey their Victorian husbands? The prescription for female hysteria was usually a good spot of doctor-administered vaginal massage until the woman achieved "hysterical paroxysm."

Yes. The cure for female hysteria was a doctor's hand down your bloomers until you were screaming his name. Is it any wonder the list of symptoms for female hysteria was so long? Doctors, astonishingly enough, grew tired of "curing" all these women. According to Rachel P. Maines's *The Technology of Orgasm*, the hand strain led doctors to invent the vibrator, and thus this section comes to a happy ending.

Brendan McGinley

FOUR GREAT WOMEN BURIED
BY THEIR BOOBS

WHILE modern women still deal with entirely too much job discrimination, domestic abuse, and sex with Gene Simmons, that's nothing compared to the old days. Back when *feminist* was a homophobic adjective and *suffrage* was what women got when dinner was cold, some ingenious voices were never heard because they just happened to be attached to a pair of breasts.

4. ROSALIND FRANKLIN

Rosalind Franklin was a pioneer in the field of genetics, whose work on unraveling the DNA double helix was largely ignored. Franklin studied at Cambridge in the 1940s, a school that didn't give women degrees at the time, figuring they wouldn't know what to do with something like an advanced biology degree—probably sew it a little suit and take it for summer constitutionals.

Still, Franklin went on to research molecular biology around the same time as Francis Crick and James Watson, the scientists credited with discovering DNA's double helix model. In fact, she wasn't far from making the discovery herself and was well ahead of Crick and Watson when her boss, Maurice Wilkins, intervened. Doing his duty as a concerned citizen, Wilkins knew he couldn't trust such valuable scientific knowledge in the hands of a mere woman—surely it was only a matter of time before she accidentally baked it into a pie!

Working behind Franklin's back, Wilkins gave her findings to Watson, who used them and Crick's LSD-spiked intuition (see page 123) to leapfrog Franklin and discover DNA's double helix pattern before her.

Their double helix model was published in an issue of *Nature* magazine, instantly making them international celebrities. Rather than acknowledging the role a woman played in the actual discovery, *Nature* published Franklin's not yet complete work in the same journal. Sure, publishing the almost-discovery of DNA's model in the same issue as the actual discovery might seem redundant, but *Nature* couldn't miss out on the adorable hilarity of a woman trying to do science. That was probably considered the monkey riding a bicycle of its day.

Buried by the boobs

In 1962, Crick, Watson, and Maurice goddamned Wilkins (whose contribution to molecular biology amounted to hating women) received the Nobel Prize in Physiology or Medicine, while Franklin received the Dick-All Prize for Diddly-Squat. Franklin's huge contribution was almost totally ignored in Watson's paper. We never thought we'd say this, but *damn you, boobs!*

3. CAMILLE CLAUDEL

Camille Claudel was a young, shockingly talented sculptress whose works are today considered masterpieces. Her career path followed the classic artist model: fabulous early works, discovery by a great mentor, total insanity, dying unloved, alone, and weird. (This is why your parents didn't let you go to art school.) But while some artists go crazy because it's the cool thing to do (we're looking at you Van Gogh), Claudel was force-fed crazy pills for her socially unacceptable lack of a penis.

In 1800s Paris, women were prohibited from studying the nude human form, because this would've ruined the wedding-night surprise. (Surprise! It's a penis.) Claudel was therefore unable to gain entry to the École des Beaux-Arts, where she would have been able to promote her work and receive commissions. In short, Claudel needed some cock in the worst way.

Luckily, her father managed to get her enrolled at the lesser Académie Colarossi, a place dedicated to the free and unbiased exploration of penises. Claudel thrived until she fell in love with Auguste Rodin, and it all went to *le toilette*.

Buried by the boobs

She became Rodin's lover and muse, influencing and reportedly even working on some of his greatest works. Meanwhile, her sculptures were shunned by the public, since no one could stomach the idea that a female might be responsible for their favorite rock penises. In fact, artistic genius in women was believed to be a form of mental illness.

After Camille broke off their relationship, Rodin switched to shafting her metaphorically, blocking all funding for her future sculptures. Claudel's own brother decided to have her committed to an insane asylum, despite the hospital's protests that Camille was totally sane for the next *thirty years*. Sadly, convinced that she would never gain recognition, Claudel ultimately destroyed the vast majority of her works. Those that survive are lauded. In the words of Ludovic Chanzy, cultural director of the Nogent museum: "That Camille was shunned by the art world, despite her beautiful work, can be explained by the fact that she was a woman. It was just not acceptable that a young lady could sculpt erotic pieces showing men and women in the nude."

That's right: People turned down free, publically viewable porn because it was made by a woman. *How far we've come . . .*

2. LISE MEITNER

Lise Meitner was the physicist who, working with Otto Hahn, pioneered the principles of nuclear fission. Meitner also discovered the Auger effect two years before Victor Auger. To add to her list of challenges, she was also an Austrian Jew in Hitler's Germany. The odds were against her, to say the least. But Meitner's biggest problem wasn't even the Nazis (that's a hell of a Jew who can say that): Berlin University was so sexist that she was only allowed to conduct experiments in a carpentry shed in the basement.

In 1938, when the Third Reich began sending subtle signs that she might want to flee for her life, she reluctantly abandoned her research with Hahn.

Buried by the boobs

Despite Meitner's crucial role in every stage of fission research, her erstwhile partner Hahn won the Nobel Prize all alone. Some of the blame in this must be apportioned to Hitler, since

he drove her out of the country, but it's not like the Nobel Foundation didn't know she existed, seeing as she had been jointly nominated with Hahn *ten times* previously. But she would have been the first woman to win a Nobel Prize without her husband, and the committee had a policy to uphold.

Jordan Monsell

1. BEATRIX POTTER

Beatrix Potter was a children's author, most known for the Peter Rabbit series. That sounds about right; that's a charming, nonthreatening, non-emasculating and totally, quaintly appropriate career for a woman.

But the bit you probably *don't* know is that she was also an absolutely brilliant mycologist, someone who studies fungi and their effects.

Anthony Clark

Since she was excluded from universities, Potter was forced to assist Scottish mycologist Charles McIntosh, illustrating his fungal specimens (which is either exactly what it sounds like or sexual innuendo was a much more dense and terrifying thing back in the day).

She became a pioneer in her field, proposing that lichens were a mixture of algae and fungus living in a symbiotic relationship, a revolutionary idea in the 1890s. She also noted that some fungi produced antibiotic chemicals, a discovery so important it shook the world . . . when it was discovered *again* by Alexander Fleming! And, hey, we just discovered it right now! And so did you! Man, science is cake!

Buried by the boobs

In 1897, Potter contributed a paper on mycology to the Linnean Society entitled "Germination of the Spores of the Agraricinae." It didn't get published. The Royal Society followed suit, scientifically cock blocking Potter at every turn. In 1901, a disheartened Potter wrote and illustrated *The Tale of Peter Rabbit* as a means of keeping her drawing skills alive. The book's unexpected success, along with the collective and multitudinous shafting from the entire scientific community, persuaded her to drop her groundbreaking work in the sciences. In 1997, the Linnean Society publicly apologized for its treatment of her. Perhaps they owe the rest of the world an apology too: Because Fleming didn't "discover" penicillin until 1928 (see page 103), a full thirty years after Potter first identified it. If Potter's work hadn't been rejected, countless lives would have been saved. On the other hand, the world would have been denied the soothing balm of Flopsy, Mopsy, and Cotton-tail. And, really, when you lay it all in the balance, which is the more effective antibiotic?

Penicillin? Fair enough. Just trying to make a point.

Winston Rowntree

THE AWFUL TRUTH BEHIND FIVE ITEMS ON YOUR GROCERY LIST

HEY, that banana you're eating? It probably killed somebody!
Well, sort of. Bananas don't kill people; people kill people . . .
over bananas. And soda. And a bunch of other stuff you buy
at the food store. For example:

5. CHIQUITA BANANAS

In 1975, Chiquita president Eli Black left the company by leaping out the window of his forty-fourth-floor office in the Pan Am Building in New York. His replacement, upon taking the reins, was quoted as saying, "It's important that I don't get too knowledgeable about the past."

What's this "past" he didn't want to think about? Well, there was the massacre of striking Colombian workers the company allegedly ordered in the twenties. But that was almost fifty years before. He was likely worried about more recent atrocities, like the CIA coup they'd orchestrated in the fifties. Yep, a freaking CIA coup. Orchestrated by a banana company.

Manuel Rebollo

The idea gets a lot less ridiculous, and way more depressing, when you know a few things: The head of the CIA in 1951, Allen Dulles, had been on the board of trustees of the United Fruit Company, which is what Chiquita was called in

1951. Around this time, Guatemala elected Jacobo Árbenz to the presidency, and Árbenz made the mistake of thinking that meant a damn thing. His plan was to purchase a small portion of United Fruit's land and distribute it to poor Guatemalan peasants.

When Árbenz hesitated to pay the company $16 million (its own internal documents valued the land at half a million), United Fruit decided this was a reasonable point in the negotiation process to ask the CIA to intervene. And *goddamn* did they intervene, replacing the freely elected Árbenz with a right-wing dictator and starting a goddamned civil war. Guatemala's brief flirtation with democracy and prosperity was over, but, hey, it's not all bad. The civil war that resulted from the coup eventually ended. In 1996.

4. NESTLÉ QUIK

For any youngster who cringes at the thought of having to choke down a glass of plain milk with dinner, Nestlé Quik is a little box of magic. One tablespoon of the powdery goodness can transform that glass of white nasty into a delectable cup of chocolaty awesome. Add to this the fact that every box is emblazoned with an adorable cartoon rabbit, and what you have is a certified childhood dream maker.

At least that's true for most kids—lazy, shiftless bastards that they are. Some kids, on the other hand, have to work for their Nestlé Quik. The majority of the world's cocoa supply comes from Africa's Ivory Coast, where child labor, trafficking, and (oh dear) slavery are not uncommon. But, hey, there's no way a corporation with such an adorable mascot would let that shit go down on its watch, right?

Well, after years of flying under the atrocity radar, word of the unspeakably harsh conditions on Ivory Coast cocoa plantations finally came out in 2001. In the face of an influx of negative publicity, Nestlé valiantly leapt into inaction. After issuing public statements claiming it had no way of knowing who did what, where, or when, the company was finally forced to acknowledge the problem by an agricultural bill that would have created a federal system to certify and label chocolate products as "slave free."

Finding its hand forced, Nestlé decided to nut up and make a claim it had no intention of following through on: to end forced labor on cocoa farms by 2005. Of course 2005 came and went with little or no change. According to Nestlé, an escalating civil war in the Ivory Coast made it too dangerous to go in and save the children. Amazingly, its team of buyers, presumably a team of crack military commandos, has yet to have a problem getting the cocoa in and out of the region.

3. IAMS PET FOOD

When PETA isn't being crazy and launching the only public-awareness campaign that people have masturbated to, it's actually been known to do some good not related to celebrity nudity. In 2002, a PETA official went undercover at an Iams testing facility and found out that, in addition to pet food, IAMS is in the business of making budding serial killers look like the kid from *Lassie*.

In case you're (justifiably) suspicious of anything tofurkey-crazed PETA members tell you, they brought back video footage of the facility that you can find on the Internet if you're ever in the mood to have your day ruined.

You really don't want to read about the most horrifying things they found. Among the less nightmare-inducing tidbits were cats and dogs gone stir-crazy from constant confinement and an employee overheard talking about a live kitten that was accidentally washed down a drain. For you statistics geeks out there, one procedure performed at the Iams facility (seriously, you don't want to know) resulted in twenty-seven dogs being killed. Just one more record Michael Vick will never break.

When confronted with PETA's findings, Iams attempted to turn the tables, claiming the undercover PETA official was responsible for the various atrocities. A review of phone transcripts revealed the exact opposite. The PETA official actually tried to prevent animal cruelty. Iams officials acknowledged this to be the case. And then presumably drowned a bag of kittens out of frustration.

2. DOLE BANANAS

Making their second appearance on the list, bananas are the standard-bearer when it comes to corporate atrocity. Following in the heinous footsteps of Chiquita, Dole has a long track record of bringing the pain to South American countries unlucky enough to grow their shit. And unlike most other companies on this list, Dole didn't even try to hide its hell-raising ways. Kudos!

When several chemical workers became sterile, tests determined the cause to be a pesticide made at the plant where they worked, called DBCP. When tests revealed it caused liver, kidney, and lung damage, the Environmental Protection Agency banned its use in the United States. Proving themselves to be a paragon of classiness, Dole made note of the "in the United States" part of the ban and continued to use DBCP overseas. When Dow Chemical informed Dole of its concerns over the safety of DBCP, Dole did what any company concerned with the well-being of its employees would do. It advised Dow it would be in breach of its contract if it refused to provide DBCP and agreed to take any liability for the resulting damage it may cause.

A brave move, agreeing to take the liability—or at least it would be if Dole thought for a second that it would ever have to act on it. See, Dole knew about a legal doctrine that would allow it to force the cases to be tried in the impossibly corrupt courts of the plaintiff's home country, so when a bunch of Nicaraguan farm workers started getting sick, Dole calculated that it would cost less to pay off Nicaraguan courts than to stop using DBCP. When that plan failed and the banana workers started winning cases, Dole moved to plan B, plugging its ears and humming loudly. So far, despite court-ordered judgments favoring Nicaraguan banana workers totaling more than $400 million, the workers have yet to see a dime.

1. COCA-COLA

The sweet bubbly deliciousness that is Coca-Cola has been a beacon of happiness for generations of kids and adults alike, even those who weren't around back when it was spiked with nose candy (see page 127). With all of this universal joy spreading, some people may be surprised to find that Coke II isn't the only atrocity in the big red machine's closet.

If you work at one of the Coca-Cola bottling plants in Colombia, South America, *dear God why?* There's a saying in Colombia that "union work is like carrying a tombstone on your back." If you spend too much time thinking about it, you'll realize that saying makes no damn sense. Just trust that unions are generally frowned upon by the armed paramilitaries who rule the Colombian streets.

But it's not like the unions didn't have it coming. They're always asking for things like fair wages and humane conditions for their workers, both of which can hurt the bottom line of global corporations thinking about housing their factories there. This in turn means less money for the Colombian government. Fortunately for global corporations, the Colombian government is corrupt as hell.

A great example of how economics works in Colombia is the Coca-Cola bottling plant in Carepa, where five union leaders were murdered between 1994 and 1996 alone. In the most publicized case (meaning not really publicized at all, unless you count the Internet, which you shouldn't), union executive board member Isidro Segundo Gil was murdered near the gates of the Coke bottling plant by paramilitary thugs.

Of course, Coca-Cola denies the assassination had anything to do with their policies. It was probably just a coincidence that a union organizer who opposed management policies was gunned down! Hell, machine-gunning someone is probably considered a sign of respect in Colombia!

In 2004, then New York City councilman Hiram Monserrate assembled a fact-finding delegation to conduct an independent investigation on behalf of his strongly Latin American constituency. After meeting with Coke officials, Monserrate's delegation travelled to Colombia and spoke with workers and eyewitnesses to the unfortunate machine-gun accidents that kept befalling unionized factory workers who opposed the bottling company's policies. After hearing both sides of the story, the delegation concluded that management had either looked the other way or actively employed paramilitary enforcers to murder union supporters.

The thing that seemed to push the delegation over the edge was the day after the murder, when eyewitnesses say the gunmen returned and forced workers to sign paperwork re-signing their union memberships. For whatever reason, Mon-serrate's fact finding delegation also seemed to take issue with the fact that Coke never bothered to conduct an investigation into a murder that was committed in a Coke bottling plant and that conveniently helped Coke's bottom line.

Of course, we can't say for sure that Coke deserves any blame for Gil's murder. Those are just allegations, made against a giant corporation with way more lawyers than Cracked.com. So, really, you shouldn't assume anything. Like the old saying goes, "When you assume, you just make an ass out of you and me and evil corporations that have rancid sucking wounds where their hearts should be."

Manuel Rebollo

FIVE CLASSIC CARTOON CHARACTERS WITH TRAUMATIC CHILDHOODS

SATURDAY-MORNING cartoons offered children of the 1980s and '90s hilarious gags, flashing colors, and lovable characters their age, some being brought up in environments so abusive they made even your crappy parents seem decent by comparison. Don't remember that last part? You must not have been paying attention to the plight of characters like . . .

5. PENNY FROM INSPECTOR GADGET

Legal guardian
Inspector Gadget, the cyborg that would have resulted if RoboCop's accident had also made him retarded.

Where are the parents?
In the world of classic cartoons, roughly 80 percent of all children are orphans. This is important because it teaches young viewers that someday their parents will mysteriously disappear from their lives for no reason and never be mentioned again. Penny was Gadget's "niece," but she looks nothing like him and shares none of his baffling incompetence.

The horror
Most episodes open with Gadget warning Penny that the mission he's about to go on is too dangerous for her (always after he's disposed of a clearly labeled explosive by carelessly tossing it in his employer's face). While these warnings might seem responsible to an outsider, Penny knows better. She *has to go*. If she doesn't save his ass from whatever malfunctioning machinery happens to spring out of it next, it's back to the orphanage.

When Gadget actually invites his

Manuel Rebollo

The gritty reboot of your childhood cartoons, starring a malnourished Dakota Fanning, Howard the Duck, and a real, terrified chipmunk.

niece to come along and match wits with a global terrorist (he does this multiple times), it's probably the most responsible thing he could do. At least she doesn't have to figure out a way to pay for airfare and travel to strange lands unaccompanied by a grown-up.

Not that her uncle is an adult in any real sense of the word. Penny probably had to start childproofing their house as soon as she could walk. But he looks like one to outsiders, and for a twelve-year-old girl constantly traveling to foreign countries by herself, kidnappers and perverts must be a constant concern.

The missions are no picnic. It turns out there's a reason that *real* detectives don't bring their kids along to investigate global terrorists. Penny is kidnapped dozens of times, and on one occasion has to be rescued from a machine designed to crush her to death. By her dog.

In fact, when you look at everything she goes through to continue living with her defective robot guardian, it becomes pretty clear what a goddamned horror show cartoon orphanages must be. Which is bad news for . . .

4. HUEY, DEWEY, AND LOUIE

Legal guardian

First their uncle, Donald Duck, then when Donald joins the navy, their great-uncle Scrooge McDuck. Apparently when you're a duck, even if you're from the same family, your last name reflects whatever crude ethnic stereotype you represent.

Where are the parents?

According to volume 1, number 1, of *Walt Disney's Comics*, the boys "hospitalized their father when a prank involving firecrackers went wrong." Historically speaking, in cartoons explosions are about as effective as laws requiring the wearing of pants. So this was either one *massive bitch* of an explosion, or the biological parents are just using it as an excuse to get away from their indistinguishable kids. Given the fact that the parents have never sought contact with them again, we're leaning toward the latter.

The horror

After being abandoned, they are left in the care of Uncle Donald, who's known for having anger-management problems. He in turn hands them off to a moneyed, distant relative four times their age who is generally thought to be an asshole by everyone in his community. So they are abandoned *twice over* before they even hit puberty.

The sheer size of Scrooge's fortune, coupled with the lack of anyone their own age to socialize with, pretty much guarantees that Huey, Dewey, and Louie will grow up to become Duckberg's version of the Gotti children, a fate that anyone outside of the hair-gel industry can agree is worse than death itself.

3. THE TEENAGE MUTANT NINJA TURTLES

Legal guardian

Master Splinter, if giant rats who live illegally in the sewers can indeed be considered "legal" anything.

Where are the parents?

Once normal turtles, the boys were transmogrified into hideous abominations after marinating in radioactive sludge, which means their parents are most likely still just normal turtles, eating wilted lettuce, scrabbling against glass walls, and humping one another for the amusement of YouTube viewers.

The horror
The real villain here is Master Splinter. OK, also Shredder. But Splinter was once a disgraced human ninja, who immigrated to New York City and immediately took up residence in the sewers rather than trying to find housing. Once the turtles arrived and he was changed into a rat, he decided the best course of action was to teach his newly adopted sons to be a noble—if hilariously in-your-face—ninja fighting squad.

Let's go over that again the way the people from Child Protective Services would put it: Known soldier of fortune Hamato Yoshi fled to the United States, likely to avoid arrest for one of his many murders. He evaded immigration authorities by living in the sewers, where he raised four young men from infancy. Throughout their upbringing, he kept them largely confined to the sewer system, fed them a steady diet of junk food, and brainwashed them into forming a code-named terrorist gang willing to enact violence on his behalf.

How Donatello ever learned to "do machines" in this environment remains a mystery.

2. KIT CLOUDKICKER FROM TALESPIN

Legal guardian
Rebecca Cunningham, owner of the Higher for Hire air-delivery business and most attractive bear on television outside of Zach Galifianakis.

FIVE CARTOON CHARACTERS WITH TRAUMATIC CHILDHOODS

Where are the parents?

Yep, another orphan. According to the show, Kit was raised by air pirates before meeting Baloo, the jocular drunk who encourages him to get towed behind airplanes while standing on a sheet of metal. If air pirates are anything like their waterborne brethren, Kit's backstory implies (a) that his parents were murdered in front of him and (b) that he's been routinely sexually assaulted (the sky, she is a lonely place).

The horror

At first blush, Kit seems to have a shot at recovering from his deep emotional scars. He's been adopted into a nice family, headed by an educated, no-nonsense woman; just the type of sexy bear lady a young tough needs to set some boundaries and turn his life around.

Unfortunately, he spends most of his time endangering his life with Baloo the flying DUI.

Also he lives in a town with only one way in or out: a tiny crack in a cliff face constantly being patrolled by the same murderous air pirates that slaughtered his parents. We have to imagine it's tough to mature into anything resembling a normal adult when your childhood is one long flashback to your parents being murdered and the filthy pirate sex that robbed you of your innocence.

1. ALVIN, SIMON, AND THEODORE

Legal guardian

David Seville, a jingle-writing lifelong bachelor in his thirties, who for some reason lives in a four-bedroom house by himself.

Where are the parents?

The show gives no hints, but assuming they're also talking chipmunks logic dictates that they're either squashed flat on the interstate somewhere or still in the woods wondering who the hell kidnapped their beloved children.

The horror

Dave illegally cares for three children (not his) and forces them to learn complicated song-and-dance numbers for his own profit. When they fail to perform to his impossible standards, he yells, "Alvin!" at them and makes them start over.

He's the ultimate weirdo stage dad.

Dave's been drinking again.

Naturally, the chipmunks are kept pantless, forced to clothe themselves in modified burlap sacks. The fact that Alvin, Simon, and Theodore never attempt to escape suggests that the entire show is an exercise in Stockholm syndrome, and the mere *existence* of the Chipettes implies an organized ring of abusive slave-parents exploiting their children for the good of the vast and powerful novelty-song industry. At least the Powerpuff Girls got superpowers.

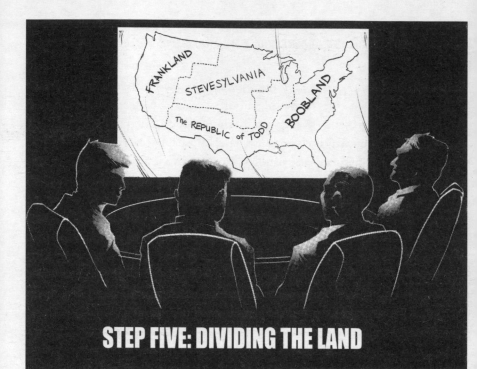

STEP FIVE: DIVIDING THE LAND

Anthony Clark

FIVE CONSPIRACIES THAT NEARLY BROUGHT DOWN THE U.S. GOVERNMENT

CONSPIRACY theorists rank alongside Scientologists and urine-soaked hobos as people you should generally not believe: 9/11 was not an inside job, vitamins don't cure everything, and that dog cannot read your thoughts. That said, it's not as if the concept of conspiracy is a purely fictional thing. In fact, there are five little-known conspiracies that many non-urine-soaked individuals believe nearly brought down the United States of America.

5. THE LINCOLN ASSASSINATION

Remember when John Hinckley Jr. tried to assassinate Ronald Reagan? Imagine how weird it would have been if he actually succeeded and if, instead of being some crazy bastard who'd seen *Taxi Driver* too many times, he'd been Robert De Niro. That's the WTF scenario Americans woke up to the morning after Abraham Lincoln was assassinated by John Wilkes Booth, one of the most famous and respected actors in the country.

The plot behind the assassination is also far stranger than your textbooks might have let on. They probably told you Booth was just a murderous lunatic with unknown motivations, rather than part of a far-reaching plan to overthrow the entire U.S. government that came terrifyingly close to succeeding.

Back then, the government was a much less stable system. If modern politics is a game of Jenga in which careful maneuvering is needed to alter even the smallest piece of legislation, then old-timey politics was also like a game of Jenga, except that it wasn't against the rules to just uppercut the whole damn stack off the table and declare yourself winner for life.

Unhappy with the outcome of the Civil War, Booth hatched a simple plot: He and his coconspirators would murder the president, vice president, general-in-chief, and secretary of state simultaneously, toppling the U.S. government so the South could rise again. And if they'd pulled it off, no safeguards were yet in place to protect the sanctity of the administration. Historian Jay Winik is of the opinion that even a simultaneous assassination of the president and vice president would have done the trick. Luckily for the United States, murderers aren't that reliable: most of the assassins chickened out, except Booth and Lewis Powell, who went to Secretary of State William Seward's home and overdosed on stab crazy, perforating Seward, the Union general guarding him, his nurse, his children, a messenger, and probably any pets that Seward had. However, the joke was ultimately on Powell: Seward survived despite dozens of stab wounds because, as Teddy Roosevelt would later prove, politicians were mostly carved from wood back then, and nothing short of a forest fire could put one down.

4. THE BURR CONSPIRACY

Aaron Burr is what is known in the political realm as a "total bastard." In 1800, he narrowly lost the presidential race to Thomas Jefferson, which he blamed on his political rival Alexander Hamilton and *not* the aforementioned bastard issue. Due to the somewhat bizarre rules of the era's politics—more *Thunderdome* than *Primary Colors*—coming in second made him the vice president, a position in which he served admirably right up until 1804, when he was informed that Jefferson was essentially firing him for his second term. Burr responded by running for governor of New York, losing, blaming Alexander Hamilton again, and then murdering him in public.

Some might consider going from being the nation's third vice president to unemployed murderer a bad year. Instead, Burr decided to embrace the supervillain role he was so clearly born to play. After murdering Hamilton, he set his sights high and began a decade-long plot with the endgame of—ready?—becoming king of the western United States. He began buying up most of Texas from the Spanish government and hiring a modest army of well-armed "farmers" to work it for him. When America went to war with Spain over the western territories, he planned to use his army to seize territory for himself. If you're thinking Burr was just a lunatic with delusions of grandeur, you should know that he had the commander in chief of the region's army and a young Andrew "Craps Thunder and Pisses Murder" Jackson on his side. If the Spanish had gotten off their lazy asses to start the Spanish-American War thirty years earlier, Texas very well could have ended up as a monarchy with Burr its first king.

He was eventually arrested for conspiracy, but, despite the best efforts of Thomas Jefferson, he was never convicted. That's not altogether surprising since he also got off for Hamilton's murder despite having shot him in a public duel witnessed by some of Hamilton's best friends. We weren't kidding around about the bastard thing.

3. MR. BUCHANAN'S ADMINISTRATION

If you think the power-crazed Burr was the highest a conspiracy ever got in the U.S. government, we'd like to introduce you to President Buchanan, who took office with one noble and lofty goal in mind: to deal with the slavery problem once and for all. It's just too bad his way of "dealing with it" was to legalize it nationwide.

Buchanan first tried to accomplish this by meddling in the landmark Supreme Court case of *Dred Scott v. Sandford*, which in 1857 set a precedent that *all* persons of African descent were to be regarded as nonhumans and therefore property. With part A of Operation Worst Goddamn President Ever accomplished, Buchanan moved on to aiding the South in its quest for secession.

That's right, the president *encouraged* secession. While Confederate skirmishes raged on unchecked in the state of

Kansas, Buchanan claimed that it was well beyond his ability to interfere in matters of secession—despite the fact that he'd just finished doing it to the Mormons in Utah. Due to his stalling, the Confederate army was able to arm itself with the stolen weaponry that made the Civil War possible. Hey, but at least he kept the Mormons from taking over Utah, right?

2. OPERATION SNOW WHITE

Sometime during the 1970s, the Church of Scientology decided its religion wasn't getting the respect it deserved. Instead of converting to a slightly less silly set of beliefs, it did what any reasonable alien-god-fearing American would: declared a covert war on the U.S. government.

The goal was basically to destroy every single sensitive document that made the religion look bad, in hopes that it would help in their prolonged war to become an officially recognized (as in tax-exempt) religion. The incredible scope of the plot came to light when two men were arrested trying to enter the U.S. Courthouse in Washington with fake IRS credentials. One of the men was sent to jail where he refused to talk, while the other, Michael J. Meisner, gave a fake name and disappeared.

According to *Time*, a year later Meisner "turned himself in, identified himself . . . and said he had just escaped from two months of 'house arrest' by cult members." He went on to describe how the church had planted employees in the IRS and Justice Department "for the express purpose of stealing documents concerning investigations of Scientology." He also said they'd broken into the IRS and planted a bug in a conference room, and stolen mind-boggling amounts of sensitive information. After humoring what they must have assumed was just a crazier-than-average Scientologist, the FBI obtained search warrants, just in case, and conducted a raid on Scientology offices that confirmed every word of Meisner's account.

Scientology's crack commandos had wiretapped and burglarized various agencies and stolen hundreds of documents, mainly from the IRS. In the end, 136 organizations, agencies, and foreign embassies were infiltrated. According to the *Phoenix New Times*, Operation Snow White was the largest infiltration of the U.S. government in history. Ever. Of the many thousand hostile governments and criminal organizations that have wanted to get their hands on sensitive U.S. intelligence, the people who actually managed to pull it off also believe that *Battlefield Earth* is a documentary.

It's impossible to say if the church was able to use information pilfered from the IRS toward its intended goal. But it's certainly strange that it didn't seem to hurt: In 1993 the IRS, the very organization it had freaking wiretapped less than fifteen years before, gave the Church of Scientology exactly what it was after, granting it recognition as an official religion. Toppling the U.S. government may not have been the stated goal, but of all the conspiracies on this list, Scientologists probably walked away from the ordeal with the most reason to believe that, should it ever become necessary, Washington, D.C., was as easy to take down as Grenada.

1. THE BUSINESS PLOT

Notice how not-fascist America is right now? It's nice, right? Well, just a few decades ago there was a plan to end this whole democracy thing, and some pretty heavy players were involved.

In 1933, a group of wealthy businessmen, which alleg-

Jordan Monsell

edly included the heads of Chase Bank, GM, Goodyear, Standard Oil, and the Du Pont family, and Senator Prescott Bush tried to recruit Marine Corps major general Smedley Butler to lead a military coup against President Franklin Delano Roosevelt and install a fascist dictatorship in the United States. And, yes, we're talking about the same Prescott Bush who fathered one U.S. president and was grandfather to another.

What went wrong? Well, as they say, never trust a man named Smedley to run your hostile military coup. Smedley was both a patriot *and* a vocal FDR supporter. Apparently, none of these criminal masterminds noticed that their prospective point man had actively stumped for FDR in 1932.

Smedley spilled the beans to a congressional committee in 1934. Everyone he accused of being a conspirator vehemently denied it, and none were brought up on criminal charges, presumably because the defendants were each independently wealthy enough to hire the Supreme Court as their legal representation. Still, the House's McCormack-Dickstein Committee deemed the general's testimony credible, before it was promptly swept under the rug of history (a gorgeous oriental number the people involved in the conspiracy paid for).

The lesson here? No matter how wealthy you are, you don't do business with guys named Smedley and you never piss off a man named Dickstein.

FOUR TICKING TIME BOMBS IN NATURE MORE TERRIFYING (AND LIKELY) THAN THE ONES IN DISASTER MOVIES

THE good news is that most of the spectacular natural disasters Hollywood and the mainstream media worry over are either exaggerated or totally made up. The bad news: nature is chock-full of ticking time bombs quietly waiting to turn the world into one of the scary books in the Bible, and you've probably never heard of any of them.

243

4. DISASTER BY LAND!

What they said to worry about: the San Andreas Fault

You may remember when Lex Luthor tried to set the San Andreas to "coast disintegrating earthquake" mode in 1977's *Superman*, or when it shook LA right off the continental shelf in the NBC miniseries *10.5*. There's even a geophysics professor who believes it will destroy LA sometime in the next decade with an earthquake he's creatively nicknamed "the Big One." While we're in no place to argue with a geophysics professor, or even know if that's a real profession, we can tell you Saint Andrew's not the guy you should be worried about.

What you should worry about: the New Madrid Fault Line

The New Madrid Seismic Zone stretches from Illinois to Alabama and doesn't care how unimpressive its IMDb page is. See, it's not in the business of destroying recognizable landmarks. It drinks terror piss and eats nightmares, and it wants to make sure America's always stocked with both.

And it can do it too.

Being underneath fly-over country makes its job easier, and not just because Alabama's sewage system was built with balsa wood and slave labor. Its landlocked location means the New Madrid can wreck your shit from five states away. Coastal towns like Los Angeles are actually *better off* in an earthquake, since a good portion of the fury gets dissipated out to sea. No such luck for anyone living in the New Madrid's million-square-mile seismic zone.

In 1968, it wrecked the civic building in Henderson, Kentucky, and made buildings sway in Boston and twenty-three other freaking states. That's pretty terrifying when you realize that the quake's epicenter was in Illinois. And that was just a blip compared to the New Madrid sequence, a series of 1811–12 quakes that registered over an 8.0 on the Richter scale (multiple times), cracked sidewalks from Missouri to Baltimore, and permanently altered the course of the Mississippi River. The few unlucky bastards already living in the Midwest at the time saw waves *rushing up rivers* and something called "sand volcanoes." Not content with claiming mere human casualties, the New Madrid took down the entire town of Little Prairie, Missouri, when it liquidated the ground it was built on. We're not exaggerating. The entire town was just swallowed by the ground. It no longer exists. Try to imagine the ground you're standing on suddenly going from solid to liquid, as though the earth, like you, was pissing itself uncontrollably. Now think about the fact that some moron took the land over the New Madrid Seismic Zone and built a large portion of America on top of it. Consider yourself warned.

3. DISASTER AT SEA!

What they told you to worry about: rogue tsunami!

In *The Day After Tomorrow*, New York City residents are blindsided when the Statue of Liberty disappears into a gray-green mist of surging seawater. *The Poseidon Adventure* opened with a rogue wave flipping a cruise ship like a bathtub toy. The actual tsunami in 2004 seemed to come out of nowhere, wiping out entire swaths of Thailand. While the causes of the real and fictional waves were all different, one thing that seems to be clear is that tsunamis can rise out of the sea without warning and ruin your shit. Hey, at least there's no sense in worrying about something we can't see coming, right? Right?

What you should worry about: the collapse of Cumbre Vieja

If a volcanic ridge in the Canary Islands falls into the Atlantic Ocean and no one is around, does it make a noise? Well, not at first. The surge of furious seawater still has to rush across the pitch black ocean floor at the speed of a fighter jet. About six hours later, however, East Coast residents would begin to hear something like a thousand freight trains rushing up out of the ocean, followed by all 110 million of their uniquely ridiculous accents merging as one to scream, "Oh shit!"

After that, not much sound.

Cumbre Vieja is a cantankerous little volcano that's erupted seven times in the last five hundred years. A group of British scientists predict that a future eruption may crack the volcano in two, sending an avalanche of rock "the size of the Isle of Man" (translated into American: Chicago) hurtling into the ocean. The resulting shockwave would reach speeds of eight hundred kilometers per hour and submerge the East Coast under fifty-meter waves (five hundred miles per hour and, "Holy shit, run!" respectively).

So Hollywood got a few details right: the Statue of Liberty being blinked out behind a surging wall of green-gray water, for instance. But it won't be some one-in-a-million rogue wave or fixable environmental selfishness. Just physics.

In everyday terms, the entire East Coast is sitting next to a pool telling the kids in the shallow end to watch their damned splashing while a giant fat guy bounces up and down on the diving board, screaming, "Cannonball!" at the top of his lungs.

2 AND 1. DISASTER FROM SPACE!

What they told you to worry about: asteroids and comets!

When discussing asteroids, comets, and other celestial debris that pass close to our planet, scientists use the bland, awkward term *near-earth objects*. In early 2009, NASA published a fourteen-page document detailing how it would stop an incoming earth smasher. The paper reads like stereo instructions, but the big points get across: we'd have plenty of warning time to pull the object away or deflect it, just like in *Armageddon*. This is the rare case where Hollywood actually proposed a reasonable solution. Probably because the really terrifying shit wouldn't make such a good movie since there's absolutely dick that we could do to stop it.

What you should be worried about: solar ejections!

Take for example, the solar ejection. It could be poor self-image, or heavy space drinking, but every once in a while the sun starts projectile vomiting. Instead of chunks of HotPockets and Jello shots, though, the sun spews radiation, often giving off the equivalent of a few million atom bombs in an hour or two. Usually, by the time the radiation reaches the earth, all that's left is a harmless light show. But in 1859, a huge so-

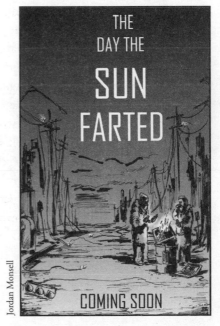

Jordan Monsell

THE DAY THE SUN FARTED

COMING SOON

lar ejection disrupted all the high technology of the day. Luckily, it was 1859, so the damage was limited to telegraph lines and countless monocles dropped in surprise. If they'd been so foolish as to build a fancy global economy that required information technology to function, power lines would have been fried, satellites destroyed, and cell phones rendered useless. It would have frozen civilization and cost trillions of dollars.

Thankfully, people in the past weren't *complete* idiots.

Oh, also: deadly gamma rays from space

When our farty little sun dies in about 5 billion years, it will expand into a sickly red dwarf that will engulf the earth in a fiery apocalypse. But there are many stars fifty to one hundred times larger than our sun that will go hypernova when they kick the bucket, spewing deadly gamma rays across the galaxy. If we're lucky, the exact right amount will hit the earth, transforming everyone into giant green-skinned monsters with anger issues.

If we're less lucky, and the wrong star explodes, it would end life as we know it. (See how unlucky that is?) Ten seconds of gamma rays could deplete half the ozone layer, allowing our sun to sneak in and fry us all to a crispy golden brown. The most likely candidate for this sunburned apocalypse is Eta Carinae—it's a scant 7,500 light-years away and scientists predict it will go boom very soon. That's less helpful than you think—on a galactic scale "very soon" could be a million years from now or tomorrow. The only thing that we really know is that when it arrives, even if every scientific community from around the globe combines forces with Bruce Willis and the worst power ballad ever written by Aerosmith, ain't shit we can do to stop it.

Winston Rowntree

FIVE PSYCHOLOGICAL EXPERIMENTS
THAT PROVE HUMANITY IS DOOMED

YOU have to be careful when you go poking around the human mind, because you can't be sure what you'll find there. A number of psychological experiments over the years have yielded terrifying conclusions, not about the occasional psychopath, but about you.

5. THE GOOD SAMARITAN EXPERIMENT (1973)

The setup

Naming their study after the biblical story in which a Samaritan helps an enemy in need, psychologists John Darley and C. Daniel Batson wanted to test if religion has any effect on helpful behavior. So they gathered a group of seminary students and asked half of them to deliver a sermon about the Good Samaritan in another building. The other half were told to give a speech about job opportunities, and members of both groups were given varying amounts of time to prepare and get across campus to deliver their sermons, ensuring some students were in more of a hurry when heading to deliver the good news.

THE TWELVE WORST TIMES

XI HEY, I WONDER WHAT HAPPENED TO THAT BLEEDING GUY ZZZZZZ
XII LUNCH RUSH
I POST-LUNCH NAP RUSH
WEB SURFING, BEATING OFF, SHOWERING, BEATING OFF RUSH
HELP?
POST-NAP WEB SURFING RUSH
TELEVISION, SHOWERING, BEATING OFF RUSH
FRENZIED "HOUR OF WORK" TO ATONE FOR PREVIOUS THREE HOURS
DINNER RUSH
STARING INTO SPACE RUSH
...THREE HOURS IN SOME PLACES
VII
WELL, IT'S MORE LIKE TWO HOURS THESE DAYS
VI
RUSH HOUR
V

TO BLEED TO DEATH IN PUBLIC!

Winston Rowntree

On the way to give their speech, the subjects would pass a person slumped in an alleyway, who looked to be in need of help.

The result

The people who had been studying the Good Samaritan story did not stop any more often than the ones preparing a speech on job opportunities. The only factor that made a difference was how much of a hurry the students were in.

If pressed for time, only 10 percent would stop to give any aid, even when they were on their way to give a sermon about how awesome it is to stop and give aid.

What this says about you

As much as we like to make fun of anti-gay congressmen who get caught gaying it up in a men's bathroom, the truth is that we're just as likely to be hypocrites. After all, it's much easier to talk to a room full of people about helping strangers than, say, to actually touch a bleeding homeless man.

And in case you thought these results were restricted to seminary students, in 2004 a BBC article reported on some disturbing footage captured by the camera of a parked public bus. In the tape, an injured twenty-five-year-old woman lies bleeding profusely in a London road, while dozens of passing motorists swerve to avoid her, without stopping.

To be fair, the report doesn't mention if there was anything good on TV that night, so they might have had somewhere really important to be.

4. THE STANFORD PRISON EXPERIMENT (1971)

The setup

You may have heard of the Stanford Prison Experiment, in which psychologist Philip Zimbardo transformed the Stanford Psychology Department's basement into a mock prison. But you probably didn't know just how ashamed it should make you to be a human being.

Seventy young men responded to a newspaper ad soliciting volunteers for an experiment. Zimbardo then gave each volunteer a test to evaluate their health and mental stability, and divided the most stable men arbitrarily into twelve guards and twelve prisoners.

Zimbardo wanted to test how captivity affects subjects put in positions of authority and submission. The simulation was planned to run for two weeks.

The result

It took less than one day for every subject to go crazier than a shit-house rat. On day two, prisoners staged a riot and barricaded their cells with their beds. The guards saw this as a pretty good excuse to start squirting fire extinguishers at the insurgents because, hey, why not?

The Stanford prison continued to ricochet around in hell for a while. Guards began forcing inmates to sleep naked on the concrete, restricting bathroom use, making prisoners do humiliating exercises and clean toilets with their bare hands. Incredibly, it never occurred to participants to simply ask to be let out of the damned experiment, even though they had absolutely no legal reason to be imprisoned.

Over fifty outsiders stopped to observe the simulation, but the morality of the trial was never questioned until Zimbardo's girlfriend, Christina Maslach, strongly objected. After six days, Zimbardo put a halt to the experiment.

What this says about you

Ever been harassed by a cop who acted like a complete douchebag for no reason? The Stanford Prison Experiment indicates that if the roles were reversed, you'd likely act the same way.

As it turns out, it's usually fear of repercussion that keeps us from torturing our fellow human beings. Give us absolute power and a blank check from our superiors, and Abu Ghraib–style naked pyramids are sure to follow. If it can happen to the sanest 35 percent of a group of hippie college students, it sure as hell could happen to you.

3. BYSTANDER APATHY EXPERIMENT (1968)

The setup

When a woman was murdered in 1964, the *New York Times* reported that thirty-eight people had heard or seen the attack but did nothing. John Darley and Bibb Latane wanted to know if the fact that these people were in a large group played any role in the reluctance to come to the victim's aid.

The psychologists invited a group of volunteers to an "extremely personal" discussion and separated them into different rooms with intercoms, purportedly to protect anonymity.

During the conversation, one of the members would fake an epileptic seizure. We're not sure how they conveyed, via intercom, that what was happening was a seizure, but we're assuming the words, "Wow this is quite an epileptic seizure I'm having," were uttered.

The result

When subjects believed that they were the only other person in the discussion, 85 percent were heroic enough to leave the room and seek help once the seizure started. This makes sense. Having an extremely personal conversation is difficult enough, but being forced to continue to carry on the conversation alone is just sad.

However, when the experiment was altered so that subjects believed four other people were in the discussion, only 31 percent went to look for help once the seizure began. The rest assumed someone else would take care of it.

What this says about you

Obviously if there's an emergency and you're the only one around, the pressure to help increases massively since you feel

100 percent responsible. But when you're with ten other people, you feel approximately 10 percent as responsible. Problem: so does everybody else.

This sheds some light on our previous examples. Maybe the drivers who swerved around the injured woman in the road would have stopped if they'd been alone on a deserted highway. Then again, maybe they'd be even more likely to abandon her since nobody was watching.

We just need the slightest excuse to do nothing.

2. THE ASCH CONFORMITY EXPERIMENT (1953)

The setup

Solomon Asch wanted to run studies to document the power of conformity, for the purpose of depressing everyone who would ever read the results.

Subjects were told they'd be taking part in a vision test. They were shown a line, and then several lines of varying sizes to the right of the first line. All they had to do was say which line on the right matched the original. The answer was objectively obvious.

The catch was that everybody in the room other than one subject had been instructed to give the same obviously wrong answer.

Would the subject go against the crowd when the crowd was clearly wrong?

HOW TO BE A REBEL

NOT ONLY ARE THERE **THREE** DIFFERENT WAYS TO DEVIATE FROM THE MASSES, BUT EACH IS A DISTINCT WORLD UNTO ITSELF:

BIKER   HIPPIE   INDIE ROCKER

BY ADOPTING ONE OF THESE VARIED AND COLORFUL LIFESTYLES YOU TOO CAN BE A NON CONFORMIST!

Winston Rowntree

The result

If three others in the classroom gave the same wrong answer, even when the line was plainly off by several inches, one in three subjects would follow the group right off the proverbial cliff.

What this says about you

Imagine how much that figure inflates when the answers are less black and white. We all laugh with the group even when we don't get the joke or doubt our opinion when we realize it's unpopular.

"Well, it's a good thing I'm a rebellious nonconformist," you might say. Of course, once you decide to be a nonconformist the next step is to find out what the other nonconformists are doing and make sure you're nonconforming correctly.

1. MILGRAM (1961) AND MILGRAM 2 (1972): ELECTRIC BOOGALOO

The setup

At the Nuremberg trials, many of the Nazis tried to excuse their behavior by claiming they were just following orders. So in 1961, Yale University psychologist Stanley Milgram conducted the infamous Milgram Experiment, testing subjects' willingness to obey an authority figure.

Each subject was told they were a "teacher" and that their job was to give a memory test to a man (actually an actor) located in another room. Subjects were told that whenever the other guy gave an incorrect answer, they were to press a button that would give him an electric shock.

As far as the subjects knew, the shocks were real, starting

at 45 volts and increasing with every wrong answer. Each time they pushed the button, the actor would scream and beg for the subject to stop.

The result

Many subjects began to feel uncomfortable after a certain point and questioned continuing the experiment. However, each time a guy in a lab coat encouraged them to continue, most subjects followed orders, delivering shocks of higher and higher voltage despite the victims' screams.

Eventually, the actor would start banging on the wall that separated him from the subject, pleading about his heart condition. After further shocks, all sounds from the victim's room would cease, indicating he was dead or unconscious. Take a guess, what percentage of the subjects kept delivering shocks after that point?

Between 61 and 66 percent of subjects continued the experiment until it reached the maximum voltage of 450, continuing to deliver shocks after the victim had, for all they knew, been zapped into unconsciousness or the afterlife.

Most subjects wouldn't begin to object until after 300-volt shocks. Exactly zero asked to stop the experiment before that point (pro tip in case you're ever faced with a similar dilemma: Under the right circumstances 110–230 volts is enough to kill a man).

The Milgram Experiment immediately became famous for what it implied about humanity's capacity for evil. But by 1972, some of his colleagues decided that Milgram's subjects must have known the actor was faking. In an attempt to disprove his findings, Charles Sheridan and Richard King took the experiment a step further, asking subjects to shock a puppy every time it disobeyed an order. Unlike Milgram's experiment, this shock was real. Exactly twenty out of twenty-six subjects went to the highest voltage.

What this says about you
Almost 80 percent. Think about that when you're at the mall: Eight out of ten of the people you see would torture the shit out of a puppy if a dude in a lab coat asked them to. And there's a good chance you would too.

THE FIVE CREEPIEST URBAN LEGENDS THAT HAPPEN TO BE TRUE

THE best creepy campfire stories are always the ones that end with the words, "It's all true, and I have the documentation here to prove it!"

In that spirit, we've tracked down five of the creepiest tales and urban legends that really happened to real people, proving once and for all that nothing is more terrifying than everyday life.

5. THE LIVING SEVERED HEAD

The legend

Your head remains aware even after it's severed from your shoulders (giving you just enough time to reflect on how stupid you were to stand up on that roller coaster).

The legend says severed heads have been known to blink and, yes, even to try to talk.

The truth

Throughout history, death by decapitation has been assumed to be instant and painless (the guillotine was designed as a humane execution method—the fact that it looked freakin' cool was a bonus) but there's evidence that your brain remains conscious anywhere from several seconds to a minute after your head gets lopped off.

One of the earliest and best-known proofs of this came from a Dr. Beaurieux, who conducted an experiment on a French murderer named Languille. Post-guillotining, Languille's eyes and mouth continued to move for five to six seconds, at which point he appeared to pass on. But then when Beaurieux shouted the subject's name, Languille's eyes popped open.

In Beaurieux's own words: "Languille's eyes very definitely fixed themselves on mine, the pupils focusing themselves," and the doctor continued to get similar results for up to thirty seconds (at which point Languille possibly just got tired of playing decapitation peekaboo).

Since modern beheadings tend not to be scheduled public events, scientists are rarely on the scene to interview a freshly chopped head. However, according to the website the Straight Dope, unlucky eyewitnesses to car accidents have reported seeing facial expressions and eye movements that seem to indicate a long moment of awareness during which the victim's detached head had time to see their own body and register whatever horrifying emotions accompany such a realization.

We did find it comforting to learn that people have taken advantage of this horrific phenomenon.

Multiple adventurers and "ethnologists" who explored the Congo basin in the late 1800s wrote about a tribe that would tie a condemned man's head to a springy sapling before chopping it off, so that the head was then catapulted into the distance after the blow. Thus their last few moments of awareness were of their head sailing breezily through the air.

If you have to die, that's got to be one of the top five ways to go.

4. THE DEADLY ELEVATOR

The legend

The metal doors clamp down on a hapless victim, who can do nothing but scream in terror as the elevator dings and begins to rise, shearing off his head or limbs as it does. It's a scene that's turned up in several cheesy horror movies. But everyone knows the doors always safely open back up when they close on your hand.

The truth

There are safety measures in place, sure. But as Dr. Hitoshi Nikaidoh learned on August 16, 2003, sometimes they don't work. Why didn't the elevator open again or shut down when the doctor became pinned between the doors at the shoulders as he was getting on? To this day, nobody knows.

On that day, the doors held Dr. Nikaidoh in place like a vise as the elevator began to ascend, until it sliced his head in two at mouth level. Find that a little nauseating? Well, try to imagine what it was like for the other person in the elevator. Yes, a nurse was in there and had to spend almost an hour in a blood-soaked box with the doctor's head.

But don't worry, according to data from the U.S. Bureau of Labor Statistics only around thirty people are killed by elevators each year. In the United States alone.

3. THE TOXIC WOMAN

The legend

A sick woman arrives at a hospital, and when the nurses withdraw blood it is so toxic that it begins making everyone around her sick too. Realizing they're dealing with the human embodiment of the creature from *Alien*, the nurses flee for their lives.

Manuel Rebollo

The truth

On the evening of February 19, 1994, Gloria Ramirez was admitted to a California emergency room, suffering from an advanced form of cancer.

When a nurse drew Gloria's blood, she detected a foul odor, so foul that hospital staff started gagging and even collapsing around her. Eventually, as many as twenty-three people were affected. The ER was evacuated and a decontamination unit brought in.

She died just forty minutes after arriving at the hospital, and her autopsy was performed by men in full hazmat moon suits. Despite one of the most extensive forensic investigations in history, it's still not known what exactly turned this woman's blood toxic. Granted, the experts on the case have refused to take off their hazmat suits since that day and are now quarantined on a small island surrounded by barbed wire, but those are probably just the usual precautions.

2. SOMETHING OFF ABOUT THAT PICTURE

The legend

A young man is dropping off groceries at the house of an eccentric old lady when he notices an old photo that makes the hair on his arms stand on end. The photo's normal enough—a young boy in his Sunday best—but something just seems off. "Isn't that beautiful?" the old lady says, trying to stuff a cat into the dishwasher. "You can hardly tell he's dead."

The truth

While most folks today are too squeamish to take more than a glance into the casket during a funeral, as recently as the early twentieth century someone dying meant it was time to break out the camera for a family photo, a practice known as memorial photography.

And, while it all sounds like the setup for some terrifying practical joke on the photographer, there was actually a somewhat reasonable explanation. Back then, taking pictures was expensive enough that it was a once-in-a-lifetime (er, or shortly thereafter) thing for most and required people to sit perfectly still for a couple of minutes. And if there's one thing dead people are good at, it's sitting still.

Eventually, the practice of memorial photography went out of style, maybe because picture taking became more affordable and didn't have to be reserved for special occasions such as death. Or possibly everyone just sat up all at once and said, "Wait, what the hell are we doing?"

1. BURIED ALIVE

The legend

Some poor schmuck is committed to his eternal resting place, even though he's not quite ready to take that final dirt nap. Scratch marks are later found on the coffin lid along with other desperate signs of escape.

The truth

This not only happened, but back in the day it happened with alarming regularity. In the late nineteenth century, William Tebb tried to compile all the instances of premature burial from medical sources of the day. He collected 219 cases of near-premature burial, 149 cases of actual premature burial, and a dozen cases where dissection or embalming had begun on a not-yet-deceased body.

This was an era before doctors such as the esteemed Dr. Gregory House gained the ability to solve any ailment within forty-two minutes (see page 205 for just how far away they were). If you showed up presumed dead, the good doctor probably leaned over your face, screamed, "Wake up!" a few times, and then buried you.

The concern over being buried alive was so real back then that the hot-ticket item for the wealthy was the "safety coffin," which allowed those inside to signal to the outside world (usually by ringing a bell or raising a flag) should they awake six feet under. Though answering that bell sounds like a good way to get ambushed by a zombie if you ask us.

And if you think you're safe, you should talk to Carlos Camejo, who got into a car accident and woke up in the middle of his autopsy. In 2007. We might suggest adding a line to your will that states you're to be buried with a gas-powered auger in your casket.

*Some historians have compared Lincoln's tone of voice to
"a howler monkey with its balls trapped in a sewing machine."*

FIVE BELOVED U.S. PRESIDENTS THE MODERN MEDIA WOULD NEVER LET INTO THE WHITE HOUSE

WASHINGTON. Jackson. Roosevelt. The tall one. Other Roosevelt. And so on. These are the men who poured the foundation for the ass-kicking spacescraper that is the United States of America. Together, they built this country with nothing but their bare hands, a fistful of stars, and an undisclosed number of dead Indians. During their presidencies, each was lauded and beloved by a majority of the nation's people.

Here's why those same beloved presidents would lose to Walter Mondale today.

5. ABRAHAM "HAMMY" LINCOLN

How beloved was he?

After naming a town after him and putting his face on two kinds of money, we apologized for the insufficient tribute by carving his face into a mountain. Then we built a body for the head and put it in a giant stone temple on prime real estate in the nation's capital. Even this was insufficient for the mighty Lincoln, so we named a log and town car after him. And thus was he sated.

Why today's media would destroy him

Even if he wasn't hideous under all that face camouflage, his voice sounded like SpongeBob's. All his transcendent, three-hour, world-changing speeches were delivered in a piercing falsetto contemporaries described as "shrill, squeaking, piping, unpleasant." Not to mention his "flesh, wrinkled and dry" or his "doughnut complexion." At the time, the ability to talk like a teakettle probably helped Lincoln's unamplified voice reach the nosebleeds. Nowadays, an annoying sound can easily torpedo a presidential campaign. If you don't believe it, just ask Howard Dean how he's been doing lately.

4. JAMES "WHERE'D 'E GO?" MADISON

How beloved was he?

Madison wrote most of the Constitution, the first ten amendments, a third of *The Federalist Papers*, and an early outline of *The Da Vinci Code*. The man had the foresight to invent the concept of checks and balances, and the balls to immediately discard them by presiding over the Louisiana Purchase as secretary of state.

You know Madison Square Garden? Guess who it's named after. Yes, for two hundred years the father of the Constitution has graced every Knicks home game, Kings of Leon encore, and WrestleMania with a sense of ancient and noble wisdom.

Why today's media would destroy him

Because he was tiny. Not just small, pixieish. At five foot four, he was the shortest man to ever hold the office, a full seven inches shorter than the presidential average, and historians are divided on whether his weight ever made it into the triple digits. Legend has it that he gave speeches from a podium made out of an old shoe box and was sworn in on a deck of cards with a cross drawn on it. He was a tiny little man is our point.

In a media landscape where

Michael Swaim

someone's gender (Hillary "No Balls" Clinton) or embarrassing flop sweat (Richard "Slimer" Nixon) can be a political death sentence, itty-bitty Madison would have been eaten alive by the likes of Rush Limbaugh (quite literally if Limbaugh mistook him for a Keebler elf). If you don't think size matters, chew on this statistic: Up to and including the election of Barack Obama, the taller of the two candidates for president has won the election 88 percent of the time. Those are betting odds, friends. It seems voters just don't cotton to a presidential candidate they can squat press.

3. GROVER "OLD NONCONSECUTIVELY" CLEVELAND

How beloved was he?

Enough to win the popular vote three times and get elected twice, nonconsecutively. That means we dumped Grover, went out with another president for a while, then came crawling back, just like he said we would in his campaign speeches and in all those sobbing voice-mail messages.

Why today's media would destroy him

He pulled a Woody Allen while in office. Cleveland married a woman twenty-eight years younger than him, whom he had helped raise from infancy, in the White House itself. While the fourth estate would have a field day with that today, that kind of thing didn't faze the sexual progressives of the 1880s, because Cleveland remained popular despite a campaign by his opponents calling out an illegitimate he'd sired while a lawyer in New York. Their unofficial slogan "Ma, Ma, where's my Pa?" was deftly countered by Cleveland's own "Gone to the White House. Kiss my ass!"

Illegitimate children? Baby wife? Man, that's what today's

media would refer to as, "Oh my God, this is so juicy I think I'm having a heart attack."

2. FRANKLIN "KING OF AMERICA" ROOSEVELT

How beloved was he?

FDR got us out of the Depression and into World War II, saving the country and inventing an entire film genre in one fell swoop. He was spawned from the ancestral loins of Teddy Roosevelt, a man who climbed the Matterhorn on his honeymoon, lost vision in one eye while boxing in the White House, and gave an hour-long speech about the fact that he had just been shot before walking onstage. Just having Roosevelt blood in your body without your veins exploding was considered pretty impressive.

All of this made him so beloved, he got elected four times. By the fourth time, it's unclear why they even bothered holding an election.

Why today's media would destroy him

Roosevelt suffered from polio, one of the most dangerous diseases of his time, and eventually died in office. If you have to be told why that wouldn't fly these days, you clearly missed the shit storm the media kicked up in 2008 about John McCain's age. And we might not have elected Obama if he hadn't promised to quit smoking. With each election, the candidate's medical records undergo more scrutiny. You think Roosevelt would have gotten away with polio, when John "Has Chunks of People Like You in His Stool" McCain can't get away with being over seventy?

Not to mention the inevitably leaked fact that Roosevelt's mother made him wear a dress until he was five.

1. JOHN "F'ED YOUR GIRLFRIEND" KENNEDY

How beloved was he?

Kennedy dealt with the Cuban missile crisis, started the Peace Corps, and won a Pulitzer Prize all while being stunningly handsome.

To put it in perspective: Kennedy was probably the most beloved president of the past thirty years. Does anyone remember where they were when they heard he got shot?

Why today's media would destroy him

He had sex with someone other than his wife while president. If you'll recall, the same thing almost ended Clinton's presidency, and all he did was play target practice with an intern in a blue dress. Furthermore, his most cited affair was with Marilyn Monroe, a huge movie star at the time. That's like if

Kennedy is still the only president to be granted jus primae noctis by popular vote.

Clinton had boned Julia Roberts. And even though rumors did swirl about JFK having affairs with other notable ladies of the era, he was never once questioned about it by the media or, for that matter, in a court of law. America sort of just said, "Boys will be boys." Perhaps we're more willing to accept a handsome man boning one beautiful woman than a chubby Southern guy rubbing one out on whoever happens to wander into his office. But Kennedy boned a different beautiful woman almost every day he was in office. Even if he gave O'Reilly sloppy seconds, there's no way Fox would let him get away with that shit.

Winston Rowntree

THIRD REICH TO FORTUNE 500: FIVE POPULAR BRANDS THE NAZIS GAVE US

IN the interest of fairness and not getting sued, we'd like to make it clear that we're not accusing any of the companies below of still being pro-Nazi. All of them have long disavowed Hitler's regime as being both monstrous and no longer profitable.

5. HUGO BOSS

No yuppie's wardrobe is complete without his standard Hugo Boss suit, shirt, tie, sunglasses, cologne, and man thong. Even if you're too poor to afford Boss's goods, you've seen Boss ads in magazines and on billboards. You know, the ones that feature serious-looking men with hollow eyes full of infinite longing that scream, "I'm attractive and I'm really very unhappy about it."

Job with the Nazis

Speaking of stern, closeted white men, Hugo Boss manufactured the sleek all-black uniforms for the Schutzstaffel (SS). While today Boss uses black for slimming effects, in the SS uniforms it was used to command respect and fear. As a bonus, the black uniforms soaked up sunlight during the summer months, causing the wearer to sweat uncomfortably and stink. Take *that*, Nazis.

How evil were they?

It's amazing how quickly Hugo Boss went from being a family owned company teetering on the brink of bankruptcy to becoming a hugely profitable juggernaut outfitting the entire Nazi army. Turns out, all you have to do is stop paying employees and introduce the motivational wonders of loaded machine guns. According to a *Los Angeles Times* report, Hugo Boss's Nazi uniforms were likely made in factories "manned by forced labor, including concentration camp prisoners and prisoners of war."

But unlike the products of some other companies on this list, the uniforms weren't directly responsible for killing people. In fact, since they actually made the wearers uncomfortable and smelly, relative to the rest of these companies Hugo Boss probably deserves a medal.

4. VOLKSWAGEN

German automaker Volkswagen came on the scene just before World War II. The company was founded by Ferdinand Porsche, the granddaddy of those fast, expensive cars that douchebags drove in the 1980s. But before all that, Porsche was lead designer of the most mass-produced car of all time: the Volkswagen Beetle.

Job with the Nazis

Porsche's partner in masterminding the Beetle: Hitler.

See, in 1934 ol' Adolf asked the German automobile industry to develop a "suitable small car" that could be used by everyone in Germany. The Beetle was Porsche's entry in the

great Nazi design-off and was apparently just what the führer had in his clown-shit insane mind. A year later, Hitler announced that thanks to Porsche, the Third Reich had been able to "complete the preliminary designs for the German *Volkswagen*" a word that is German for "people's car."

How evil were they?

The Beetle is perhaps the most misunderstood car in history. People look at its rounded shape and anthropomorphic face and instantly think of love and peace. In reality, it was designed to Hitler's specifications and, according to the German magazine *Der Spiegel*, manufactured with the famous Nazi work ethic, known outside of the Third Reich as "Jews from concentration camps and prisoners of war."

You have to give credit to Porsche for designing a car so impossibly cute that we forget it was brought into this world by the worst thing that ever happened.

3. IBM

IBM is one of the few IT companies whose history dates back to the nineteenth century. On one hand, this means it has been a Fortune 500 company since 1924. On the other, over a century of history gives you a lot of opportunities to make some monstrous PR blunders.

Job with the Nazis

You're probably thinking, "IBM is American! The closest America ever got to the Nazis was when Indiana Jones wore that uniform as a disguise in *Raiders*!"

Actually, prior to the war American business took what can be generously described as a morally ambivalent stance on Nazi enthusiasm for an Aryan master race. However, once the war started most American businesses disavowed Hitler's regime. IBM, on the other hand, decided to stick around and see where he was going with this whole "final solution" thing.

Back in those days, the only way to keep track of huge databases was with an extremely complicated system involving punch cards, and IBM was the best at constructing and maintaining those databases. Its databases could keep track of anything: financial ledgers, medical records, Jews . . .

Winston Rowntree

As soon as the Nazis invaded a country, they would overhaul the census system using IBM punch cards and use them to track down every Jew, Gypsy, and any other non-Aryan on record.

How evil were they?

The unabashedly anticorporate documentary *The Corporation* shows actual footage of IBM punch cards used in prison camps. They tracked people based on their religion, their location, and even how they'd be executed. For instance, Prisoner Code 8 was Jew, Code 11 was Gypsy. Camp Code 001 was Auschwitz; Code 002 was Buchenwald. Status Code 5 was execution by order, and Code 6 was gas chamber.

IBM claims it was a victim of circumstance. It had a subsidiary in Germany before Hitler took over, and the company just fell under Nazi control, like every other company over there.

But the records suggest that's not the whole truth. IBM sent internal memos in its New York offices acknowledging that its machines were making the Nazis more efficient, and it made no efforts to end the relationship with the German branch.

2. BAYER

Bayer, the massive pharmaceutical company that's most famous for making aspirin, is also behind such wonder drugs as Levitra and heroin (see page 207).

Job with the Nazis

As unpopular as heroin turned out to be with everyone besides jazz musicians, it's got nothing on the Bayer-produced Zyklon B gas, the stuff that killed millions of people in the camps. Bayer was once part of a large conglomerate, IG Farben, that churned out thousands of killer Zyklon B canisters. The gas was originally invented by Fritz Haber, a man whose life is so incredibly pathetic that you'd almost feel sorry for him, if he hadn't indirectly caused millions of deaths.

After he oversaw one of the deadliest uses of chemicals in warfare up to that point in history, his wife killed herself in their garden in protest. Then Hitler took over, and Haber decided to renounce Judaism to fit in, only to be told that he was still Jewish according to the Nazi rule book. He died of a heart attack while fleeing the country he spent his life serving, and the chemical he originally invented to kill insects was used to kill a number of his relatives. Also, he was named Fritz, so there was probably a lot of teasing on the playground.

How evil were they?

On one hand, the company that actually manufactured the gas was just partially owned by IG Farben, and Bayer was just one part of IG Farben. On the other, Bayer at one time sponsored a scientist by the name of Josef Mengele, thus facilitating his important work in the field of being the living embodiment of the evil scientist.

1. SIEMENS

Siemens AG is the massive global conglomerate that makes everything from circuits to wind turbines to maglev trains. It has almost half a million employees worldwide and is listed on every stock exchange imaginable. The company had its roots back in the nineteenth century, when famed scientist Werner von Siemens got tired of discovering stuff and decided to make some money instead. While Siemens died well before the 1940s, the company he gave his name to is so evil it may as well have its corporate headquarters inside a dormant volcano.

Job with the Nazis

Siemens struggled in the wake of World War I and the Great Depression. When Hitler rose to power in the 1930s, the Siemens executives decided things were on the upswing and started building factories near the homey neighborhoods of Auschwitz and Buchenwald.

Like Hugo Boss and Volkswagen, its wartime resurgence was fueled by Nazi Germany's version of a government bailout: cheap slave labor. But being near two of the biggest concentration camps put Siemens in position to milk the atrocity for more war-crime-fueled profit than anyone else.

Hundreds of thousands of slave workers were employed to build all sorts of goodies for the German military to use on both the western and the eastern fronts. Though it wasn't the only company at the time supplying the German war effort, it was certainly the most prolific. Siemens was in charge of Germany's rail infrastructure, communications, power generation—the list goes on.

How evil were they?
At the height of the Nazi terror during the 1940s, it was not atypical for a worker to build electrical switches for Siemens in the morning and be snuffed out in a Siemens-made gas chamber in the afternoon.

A few years ago, in an act of insensitive assholery so colossal it could blot out the sun, Siemens tried to trademark the name Zyklon with the intent of marketing a series of products under it. Including gas ovens.

This raises a few questions about Siemens's business practices, most significantly, "What the hell is wrong with you people?"

FIVE SCIENTIFIC REASONS WHY A ZOMBIE APOCALYPSE COULD ACTUALLY HAPPEN

OUR culture is full of tales of the undead walking the earth, from the New Testament to our comic books. But a zombie apocalypse isn't actually possible, right?

Right?

Guys?

Actually, it's quite possible. Here are five ways it could happen, according to science.

5. BRAIN PARASITES

What are they?

Parasites that turn victims into mindless, zombielike servants are fairly common in nature. There's one called *Toxoplasma gondii* that seems to devote its entire existence to being terrifying.

This bug infects rats but can only breed inside the intestines of a cat. Knowing that it needs to get the rat inside the cat, the parasite takes over the rat's brain and makes it scurry toward the cats. The rat is being programmed to get itself eaten, and it doesn't even know it.

Of course, those are just rats, right?

How it can result in zombies

Hey, did we mention that half the humans on earth are infected with toxoplasmosis and don't know it? Maybe you're one of them. Flip a coin.

If your coin just landed braaaains-side up, you should know that studies have shown that the infected will often see a change in their personality and are more likely to go insane.

Chances this could cause a zombie apocalypse

Humans and rats aren't all that different. It's why we use them to test our medications. All it would take to cause a zombie apocalypse is a more evolved version of toxoplasma that could do to us what it does to the rats. So imagine if half the world suddenly had no instinct for self-preservation or rational thought. Even less than they do now, we mean.

If you're comforting yourself with the thought that it may take forever for such a parasite to evolve, you're forgetting about all the biological weapons programs around the world busy weaponizing such bugs. You've got to wonder if those lab workers don't carry out their work under the unwitting command of the *Toxoplasma gondii* already in their brains. If you don't want to sleep at night, that is.

Granted, these people have never been dead and thus don't fit the exact definition of *zombies*, but we can assure you that the distinction won't matter a whole lot once the groaning hordes are clawing at your windows.

4. NEUROTOXINS

What are they?

There are certain kinds of poisons that slow your bodily functions to the point that you'll be considered dead, even to a doctor. The poison from Japanese blowfish can do this.

The victims can then be brought back under the effects of a drug like stramonium (or other chemicals called alkaloids) that leave them in a trancelike state with no memory but still able to perform simple tasks like eating, sleeping, moaning, and shambling around with their arms outstretched.

How it can result in zombies

Can? How about *does*.

This has already happened in Haiti, where the word *zombie* comes from. Just ask Clairvius Narcisse. He was declared dead by two doctors and buried in 1962. They found him wandering around the village eighteen years later. It turned out the local voodoo priests had been using alkaloid-like chemicals found in jimsonweed (or as it's known in Haiti, zombie's cucumber) to zombify people and put them to work on the sugar plantations.

So the next time you're pouring a little packet of sugar

into your coffee, remember that it may have been handled by a zombie at some point.

Chances this could cause a zombie apocalypse
On the one hand, it's already happened, so that earns it some street cred. But even if some evil genius intentionally distributed alkaloid toxins to a population to turn them into a shambling, mindless horde, there is no way to make these zombies aggressive or cannibalistic.

Yet.

3. THE REAL RAGE VIRUS

What is it?
In the movie *28 Days Later*, it was a virus that turned human beings into mindless killing machines. In real life, we have a series of brain disorders that do the same thing. They were never contagious, of course. Then mad cow disease came along. It attacks the cow's brain, turning it into a stumbling, mindless attack cow.

And when humans eat the meat . . .

How it can result in zombies
When humans are infected with mad cow, they call it Creutzfeldt-Jakob disease. Check out the symptoms:

- Changes in gait
- Lack of coordination (stumbling and falling)
- Muscle twitching
- Myoclonic jerks or seizures
- Rapidly developing delirium or dementia

The sanest guy in the office.

Sure, the disease is rare and the afflicted aren't known to chase after people in murderous mobs. But it proves widespread brain infections of the rage variety are just a matter of waiting for the right disease to come along.

Chances this could cause a zombie apocalypse

If the whole sudden, mindless violence idea seems far-fetched, remember that you are just one brain chemical (serotonin) away from turning into a mindless killing machine. All it would take is a disease that destroys the brain's ability to absorb that one chemical, and suddenly it's a real-world *28 Days Later*.

So imagine such an evolved disease, which we'll call super mad cow, getting a foothold through the food supply. Say this disease spreads through blood-on-blood contact, or saliva-on-blood contact. Now you have a rage-type virus that can be transmitted with a bite.

With one bite, you're suddenly the worst kind of zombie: a fast zombie.

2. NEUROGENESIS

What is it?

You know all the controversy out there about stem cell research? Well, the whole thing with stem cells is that they're basically used to regenerate dead cells. Particularly of interest to zombologists is neurogenesis, the method by which stem cells are used to regrow dead brain tissue.

How it can result in zombies

Science can pretty much save you from anything but brain death; doctors can swap out organs, but when the brain turns to mush, you're gone. Right?

Not for long. They're already able to regrow the brains of comatose head-trauma patients to the point that they wake up and walk around again. Couple that with the ability to keep a dead body in a state of suspended animation so that it can be brought back to life later, and soon we'll be able to bring back the dead, as long as we get to them quickly enough.

That sounds great, right? Well, a German lab dedicated to "reanimation research" has looked into the process of "re-animating" a person and found a small problem. It causes the brain to die off from the outside in. The outside being the cortex, the part that makes humans human. You don't need the cortex to survive, so that just leaves the part that controls basic motor function and primitive instincts behind.

So you take a brain-dead patient, use these techniques to regrow the brain stem, and you now have a mindless body shambling around, no thoughts and no personality, nothing but a cloud of base instincts and impulses.

That, ladies and gentlemen, is what we like to call a real, live, undead zombie.

Chances this could cause a zombie apocalypse

Under every legal system in the world, all rights and respon-sibilities are terminated at death. All it would take for the clock to strike "Ah, zombies!" is someone with resources and a need for a mindless workforce of totally obedient slave labor.

1. NANOBOTS

What are they?

A technology that science engineered to make you terrified of the future. We're talking about microscopic, self-replicating robots that can invisibly build—or destroy—anything. Sure, at some level scientists know nanobots will destroy mankind. They just can't resist seeing how it happens.

How it can result in zombies

Scientists have already created a one-cell nanocyborg, by fusing a tiny silicone chip to a virus. The first thing they found out is that these cyborgs can still operate for up to a month after the death of the host. Notice how nanoscientists went right for zombification, even at this early stage.

According to studies, within a decade they'll have nanobots that can crawl inside your brain and set up neural connections to replace damaged ones. That's right; the nanobots will be able to rewire your thoughts. What could go wrong?

Chances this could cause a zombie apocalypse

Do the math, people.

Someday there will be nanobots in your brain. Those nanobots will be programmed to keep functioning after you die. They can form their own neural pathways and use your brain to keep operating your limbs after you've deceased and, presumably, right up until you rot to pieces in midstride.

Of course, when that happens the nanobots would just need to transfer to a new host. Therefore, the last act of the nanobot zombie would be to bite a hole in a healthy victim, letting the nanobots stream in and set up camp in the new host. Once in, they can shut down the part of the brain that resists (the cortex) and leave the brain stem intact. They will have added a new member to the unholy army of the undead.

Look, we don't want to create a panic here. All we're saying is that on an actual day on the actual calendar in the future, runaway microscopic nanobots will end civilization by flooding the planet with the cannibalistic undead.

Science says so.

CREDITS

Nathan Birch (The Ten Most Insane Medical Practices in History, The Five Creepiest Urban Legends That Happen to Be True). In addition to working for Cracked.com, Nathan spends his time writing for top video game sites, producing his own Web comic (www.zoologycomic.com), and hoping he'll never actually have to grow up.

    Robert Brockway (Three Colors You Don't Realize Are Controlling Your Mind) is an editor and columnist for Cracked.com and the author of *Everything Is Going to Kill Everybody: The Terrifyingly Real Ways the World Wants You Dead*, a book that is infinitely superior to this one in every way. He is also fired, just now.

    Adam Tod Brown (Five Horrifying Food Additives You've Probably Eaten Today, The Awful Truth Behind Five Items on Your Grocery List) is a freelance editor and comedy writer with skills often described as "ninja-like." He holds a master's degree in street knowledge and drinks from only the finest bejeweled goblets.

    Tim Cameron (The Six Most Terrifying Foods in the World, Four Great Women Buried by Their Boobs) goes by his middle name Niall as a musician, since it's over 70 percent more pretentious. You can experience Niall's stirringly resonant soundcrafts at www.niall-cameron.com

    Erica Cantin ("Michael Bay Directs the News" in Five Stories The Media Doesn't Want You to Know About) lives in a formerly abandoned castle near the sea, where she and her family sing many a merry shanty.

CREDITS

Rory Colthurst (Five Wacky Misunderstandings That Almost Caused a Nuclear Holocaust) is a politics student based in London. He started writing when the school system would no longer let him draw pictures, and has never looked back.

Travis Corkery (Six Terrifying Things They Don't Tell You about Childbirth) is a writer from Anchorage, Alaska. He lives with his wife, Charlene, dog, Volta, and two children, one of which was conceived to research the article that appears in this book.

S. Peter Davis (The Five Most Ridiculous Lies You Were Taught in History Class, Four Mythological Beasts That Actually Exist) in addition to this sort of thing, churns out reams of unpopular and socially disturbing fiction. He lives alone in Brisbane, Australia, with his two fish, Salmon Rushdie and Marlin Brando.

Jacopo della Quercia (Numbers 5 to 3 of Five Conspiracies That Nearly Brought Down the U.S. Government) was born to Italian parents, studied Renaissance history in Florence, has taught classes on Dante, Machiavelli, and Renaissance art, believes the past is still alive, writes in code, and died in 1438.

Ben Dennison (The Four Most Insane Attempts to Turn Nature into a Weapon) writes comedy to pay the bills. The bills usually win, but hey, man, that's cool.

Justin Droms (Oh the Places You'll Go [When You're Dead]: Six Insane Things Science Might Do with Your Cadaver) was an editor at Cracked.com for two-and-a-half blood-soaked years. He currently "works" in "marketing" in Washington, D.C.

Robert Evans (Four Things Your Mom Said Were Healthy That Can Kill You, Five Stories the Media Doesn't Want You to Know About) has dedicated his life to finding every dick joke in the history of literature.

Tomas Fitzgerald (Five Scientific Reasons a Zombie Apocalypse Could Actually Happen) hails from Western Australia, the savage hell-scape that inspired *Mad Max: Beyond Thunderdome*. When

CREDITS

he's not wearing hats adorned with crocodile teeth, Tomas lectures in law at the University of Notre Dame.

Ian Fortey (Five Awesome Places to Have Sex [and the Horrific Consequences]) is a freelance writer, Cracked.com columnist, and Pisces. He will sleep on your sofa if you let him.

Alexandra Gedrose (Five Psychological Experiments That Prove Humanity Is Doomed) has a strong aversion to bottled water.

Gladstone (Five Famous Artists Who Didn't Create Their Signature Creation) is a columnist for Cracked.com and the creator and star of the popular Hate by Numbers video series. His Web site is www.KafkaMaine.com—and stay for awhile?

Christina Hsu (Five Hollywood Adaptations That Totally Missed the Point) is extremely proud of having written part of a book, which she hopes will be the first small stepping stone to her life goal of someday, possibly, if all the stars align, writing half of a book.

Peter Hildebrand (Numbers 1 and 2 of Five Conspiracies That Nearly Brought Down the U.S. Government) is a student, freelance writer, and minister (technically).

David King (Third Reich to Fortune 500: Five Popular Brands the Nazis Gave Us) is a world-renowned expert at the art of being mediocre. When he's not being sorta-funny at parties or hitting on chicks who think he's "pretty cool," he's busy being so-so in university.

Ben Joseph (Four Ticking Time Bombs in Nature More Terrifying and Likely Than the Ones in Disaster Movies) is a writer and producer on staff at CollegeHumor.com. He's also had his work published by McSweeney's and written for the upcoming Cartoon Network sketch show based on *MAD* magazine, which kind of makes him a traitor, don't you think?

Richard Kane (The Six Most Depressing Happy Endings in Movie History) has been writing Internet comedy since he was sixteen years old. He lives in California with his family.

Jeff Kelly (Five Movies Based on True Stories [That Are Complete Bullshit]) graduated from Syracuse University in 2003, is happily married to his wife, Sara, and enjoys Mexican beer, shiny things, and fighting crime. Well, most of it anyway.

Stuart Layt (The Gruesome Origins of Five Popular Fairy Tales) is a journalist and writer from Australia. With the publication of this book, he is now a "professional comedian" and will become insufferable at parties.

Alex Levinton (The Five Most Horrifying Bugs in the World, The Six Cutest Animals That Can Still Destroy You). It remains unproven whether Alex Levinton is in reality a glass jar filled with bees. About him, there is nothing more to say.

Daniel O'Brien (The Four Most Badass Presidents of All Time, Five Famous Inventors Who Stole Their Big Idea) is the senior writer of and a columnist for Cracked.com. His Web series, Agents of Cracked, is available on every Internet.

Jack O'Brien (Introduction, The Four Greatest Things Ever Accomplished While High) is editor in chief of Cracked.com, and tries not to talk too much about how Cracked.com was better "back before everyone liked it and it was still all about the music, man." He is mostly successful.

Colm Prunty (The Six Most Depressing Happy Endings in Movie History) learned to read and write by examining the backs of household cleaning products. His early writing was known to kill 99 percent of germs.

Tom Reimann (Five Fun Things That Will Kill You) was a nerdy high school student when he was bitten by a radioactive spider and contracted leukemia. He is a freelance editor for Cracked.com.

Ned Resnikoff (Numbers 1 and 2 of Five Conspiracies That Nearly Brought Down the U.S. Government): a Philosophy major at New York University, a writer, a lit nerd, a lapsed Jew, and a politics junkie.

CREDITS

Levi Ritchie (The Five Most Frequently Quoted Bullshit Statistics) is a college student from west central Texas who is passionate about writing, because it helps support his gaming addiction.

Seanbaby (Five Fight Moves That Only Work in Movies) invented being funny on the Internet, and like all writers, he was soon replaced with videos of kitty cats. But their time is coming.

Michael Swaim (Five Awesome Things You Didn't Know Could Make You Sick, Five Classic Cartoon Characters with Traumatic Childhoods, Five Beloved U.S. Presidents the Modern Media Would Never Let into the White House) is cofounder of Those Aren't Muskets! and the host of Cracked TV and Does Not Compute. As Cracked.com's Head of Video, he only dimly understands the object you are currently holding.

Brian Thompson (Five Stories about Jesus's Childhood They Had to Cut from the Bible [to Avoid an NC-17 Rating]) is an aspiring writer from Minneapolis, Minnesota. He is currently writing a novel that will be on store shelves as soon as the devil gets the paperwork for his soul in order.

Brian Walton (Five Ways Your Brain Is Messing with Your Head) spends his time in Florida alligator fishing and trying to live to regret the things he does. Like alligator fishing.

David Wong (Four Brainwashing Techniques They're Using on You Right Now, Five Scientific Reasons Why a Zombie Apocalypse Could Actually Happen) is the senior editor of Cracked.com and the author of the horror novel *John Dies at the End*, currently available everywhere except the seventy-two countries in which it has been banned.

Illustrators

Matt Barrs (illustrations on pages 51, 104, 138) is a cartoonist and comedian living in Los Angeles, where he regularly collaborates with Cracked.com on art and video projects.

CREDITS

Robert Bogl (illustrations on pages 21, 27, 108, 147, 265, 270) is an up-and-coming artist who hopes to one day create something more popular than *Star Wars*. However, he doesn't want to milk and destroy his creation like George Lucas did.

Anthony Clark (illustrations on pages 7, 13, 17, 20, 41, 47, 49, 54, 56, 60, 94, 97, 100, 123, 126, 130, 131, 136, 146, 151, 159, 176, 180, 218, 236, 280, 284) is a cartoonist and illustrator from Indianapolis. You can find more of his art, comics, and hidden torpedo launch codes at nedroid.com.

Ben Driscoll (illustrations on pages 205, 209) makes *Daisy Owl*, the world's foremost comic about a speaking owl that raises human children. He lives in San Diego with his cat.

Val Gallardo (illustrations on pages 145, 193) is a French-born illustrator living in Belgium. She loves drawing, worships Morrissey, and has a coffee addiction.

Christopher Hastings (illustrations on pages 102, 117) is the creator of *The Adventures of Dr. McNinja*, a comic that has been online since 2005. He lives in Brooklyn with his fiancée, Carly, and dog, Commissioner Gordon.

Randall Maynard (illustration on page 71) is a graphic designer based out of a secret fortress in Los Angeles, California. His free time is spent playing video games and mixing the perfect soundtrack in preparation for the zombie apocalypse.

Brendan McGinley (illustrations on pages 156, 197, 204, 213) writes comics and tells jokes in New York City. He is the terror of the Internet at brendanmcginley.com.

Jordan Monsell (illustrations on pages 1, 5, 34, 35, 73, 79, 87, 116, 155, 157, 166, 168, 184, 189, 217, 242, 247, 258) was born in New York and now resides in Los Angeles. He illustrates the Web comic *Alyster & Buttercup*, performs Shakespeare, and hikes the trails of Griffith Park.

CREDITS

Shannon O'Brien (illustration on page 22) is an interaction designer and illustrator living in Brooklyn, New York.

Brian Patrick (illustration on page 86) is the creator of Akimbo Comics.

Manuel Rebollo (illustrations on pages 221, 228, 229, 234, 261) also goes by elgatoazul and is a freelance graphic designer and illustrator based in Salamanca, Spain.

Winston Rowntree (illustrations on pages 9, 28, 29, 31, 38, 62, 63, 64, 91, 109, 111, 114, 141, 162, 169, 171, 183, 191, 206, 220, 243, 249, 250, 254, 272, 274, 276) is known for his overly verbose online comix, which can be found at viruscomix.com. In the real world he can be found in Toronto, Canada, slightly west of downtown.

Michael Swaim (illustration on page 267) is made of lasers and hate. Once he tried to get into a kid's pool party, and they wouldn't let him in. Yeah he draws, too. Now he's just showing off.